Edmonton Exhibition

Copyright 1979 Tony Cashman

Published by the Edmonton Exhibition Association
Edmonton Northlands
Edmonton, Alberta

H. K. (Harv) Haugen
Project Co-Ordinator for Public Relations Committee

Jacket design by Dale Austin
(Graphic Design and Communications Ltd.)

Printed by Bulletin-Commercial Printers Ltd. Edmonton

Bound by Atlas Book Bindery (1961) Ltd. Edmonton

I.S.B.N. 0-920564-03-8

Edmonton Exhibition the first hundred years

TONY CASHMAN

A Message From The President

It is a true privilege to be associated with the outstanding citizens who have been president of the Edmonton Exhibition in the first hundred years. One of my first memories, as a very small child, is of running away from home to look for Borden Park and the grounds where I knew I would find adventure and excitement.

We have had other exciting times in Edmonton. For me the most magnificent occasion was the Commonwealth Games, which was the climax of years of volunteer planning. It is gratifying that the Exhibition, for a hundred years, has been conducted on the same volunteer principle as the Games. Though many things have changed this remains the same. We now have twenty-six directors, all volunteers, representing every activity in the city and surrounding country, dedicating uncounted hours to building one of the largest community organizations in Canada.

Starting our second century we, and our dedicated staff, must cope with the challenge of maintaining old ideals in rapidly-changing times. It will not be easy, but looking back on the first century we have found that the Association has seldom been free of challenge or controversy or achievement either. Before going onwards, we wanted to record the progress of the first hundred years and honor those who made it possible. We agreed that the story must be told by someone who had no connection with the Exhibition but a long association with Edmonton. Tony Cashman was invited to produce the history in his own way with no editorial control by the Exhibition board. This he has done. We hope the next hundred years will produce a similar record of progress.

Sincerely,

The Chapters

1 1879

This is the scene of the first exhibition. Fort Edmonton of the fur trade dominates the shoulder of high ground where government buildings of the province of Alberta will rise later. The first exhibition was held on this site on October 15, 1879.

Livestock was shown in the stockade; grain and vegetables and women's handiwork in the Big House, home of Chief Factor Richard Hardisty, just above the fort on the left.

Exactly one week later, on October 22, 1879, the scene was photographed by George Mercer Dawson, famed trailblazer, leader of a party making the Geological Survey of Canada. Dawson's camera was set up in a clearing above present day Kinsmen Park. In the foreground, in among the trees from which Blackfoot Indians once attacked the fort with flaming arrows, is the home of John Walter, only resident south of the river. The steamer *Northcote,* first on the upper North Saskatchewan, is pulled up on the bank to ride out the winter.

On the horizon beyond the fort, very low on the horizon, lie the buildings of the Edmonton settlement.

7

Satisfaction at having a picture taken so close to the first exhibition day is constrained only by a twinge of sorrow that Mercer couldn't have had his camera pointed on the great day itself — when it would have caught some of the crowd. A large portion of the 275 residents of Edmonton, St. Albert, Fort Saskatchewan (and farms in between) were milling about the grounds that day.

Some confusion has been caused by the name of the sponsoring body: the Edmonton Agricultural Society. Membership included residents of all three settlements and the president was the founder of Fort Saskatchewan, Inspector W. D. Jarvis of the North West Mounted Police. The men in red coats had several mandates on the prairies. One was *maintaining the right*. Another was the encouragement of agriculture, in which cause they brought livestock and seeds on their westwards trek of 1874. Although Jarvis was president of the society he was not popular among all residents of Edmonton. In 1875 he had arrived with orders to build a police establishment at Edmonton House. But he had decided that the centre of population would grow where a transcontinental railroad crossed the North Saskatchewan River and it wouldn't be at Edmonton.

The location on high bluffs, chosen to discourage Indian attackers would, he felt, be equally discouraging to railroad builders and they would cross downstream where the cliffs were lower. He chose the most likely site and called it Fort Saskatchewan, and the first contract of the steamer *Northcote* was hauling building supplies for the rival settlement.

The vice-president (and host) was Chief Factor Richard Hardisty, and this too is historically interesting because only twenty years before, his employer, the Hudson's Bay Company, was assuring anyone who would listen that the prairies were frozen the year round and of no use for agriculture.

There were three directors: Sergeant-Major Belcher of the Mounties, and two gentlemen who had come originally seeking gold: Tom Lamoreaux of the Sturgeon River settlement and Donald Ross, Edmonton's first hotel man. Another ex-prospector left the Fort with three of the 173 dollars offered in prize money, two for the best fat ox and one for the third-best turnip. He was "English Charlie". Charlie Stevenson lived on Miner's Flat, now Laurier Park and site of the Valley Zoo. He still panned gold as he had all his adventurous life but was into agriculture as well. Charlie attended all the big gold rushes — California in '49, the Cariboo in '58. When he wandered over the mountains into Alberta he once saved himself from a winter storm by sheltering inside a buffalo. Caught by the blizzard Charlie shot a buffalo, cleaned out the insides and climbed in until the danger passed. So when an adventurer like English Charlie set out to prove the gentle possibilities of agiculture he showed encouraging faith in the country.

Malcolm Groat, another with faith in the country, went home a winner — to his home on a land claim still known as Groat Estate. Malcolm was the first Hudson's Bay man to retire in Edmonton after his twenty-year service rather than go home to Scotland. He was awarded three dollars for the best yoke of oxen, two for finest pumpkin and four for the best potatoes. And the prize goobers were selected from 13 hundred pounds of potatoes grown on 2¼ acres, mostly of fresh-broken sod. Frank Oliver made a feature of this last point in his report to the Saskatchewan Herald. Frank had not yet founded the Edmonton Bulletin — he was waiting for the press to come by Red River cart — but he was firing off enthusiastic broadsides to the nearest newspaper, published at Battleford. A serving employee of the Hudson's Bay Company, Mr. Taber, walked off with one-sixth of the prize money — 31 dollars in all. Mr. Taber took the ten-dollar first award for wheat — the Governor's prize presented personally by the Lieutenant-Governor of the Territories. He also won three dollars for best rye, three dollars for best peas, two dollars for second-

The founders: Hardisty and Jarvis

best potatoes, two dollars for best tomatoes, one dollar for second-best cabbage, one dollar for second best onions, two dollars for best celery, and five dollars for best collection of vegetables — plus two dollars worth of seeds donated by the Saskatchewan Herald.

The king of corn, John Coleman, didn't win any money for his prize effort in corn — just a year's subscription to the Herald.

There were nine divisions in the women's part of the fair. Most appealing among that first list of handiwork was the embroidered leather — put in by three Indian girls married to white men of the Edmonton district. Their total prize money was ten dollars.

There weren't as many ladies present as the sponsors had hoped for, because the weather had turned threatening that October day. There wasn't as much grain in the show as the sponsors had hoped for, because there were only two threshing machines in the district and both had broken down. And there wasn't as much livestock as the sponsors had hoped for, because many growers had declined to invest the necessary dollar. And the vegetables were past their peak — some of them had gone to seed.

Still, with all these drawbacks, the first exhibition was reported a resounding success by correspondent Frank Oliver. He wrote:

"Few persons in this neighbourhood had ever seen, nor did they understand, the use or nature of an exhibition; some say they did not exhibit because they knew their neighbor had better than they had; others feared to invest a dollar for membership, lest it might by thrown away. But since the exhibition, those who did not make an entry are sorry for it, and nearly all are convinced that there is no better way to improve farm produce and show to the world the peculiar fertility of our soil, than by supporting an agricultural society."

2 1979

What a difference a hundred years can make. This is Northlands, 126.56 acres, home of the fair in centennial 1979, dates July 20 to 28. Much has happened since George Mercer Dawson photographed Fort Edmonton. The invention of the airplane is an obvious feature. Development of the motor car is another. Not so obvious is the Ferris wheel, introduced at the Chicago World's Fair of 1893. When night falls yet another advance of the intervening century will be revealed.

Centennial contrast can be dramatized by the photographer. A rare opportunity is also presented the statistician, a fellow who seldom gets an exciting story to tell. Here's his chance, comparing 1879, a single event on a single day, to 1979, some 15 hundred activities covering all days of the year.

The statistician may well start with attendance. For 1879 he'll estimate a generous portion of 275, the entire population of Edmonton, St. Albert and Fort Saskatchewan. For 1979 one million people for the fair, plus two million for other events.

In 1879 there was one event-day; a century later 1,371 event-days superimposed on 365 calendar days. The oldest building on the grounds, the Gardens, dated 1913 and spanning two-thirds of the century, will still be rented on 222 days. In winter it will be booked for hockey from six a.m. to midnight every day but Christmas and New Year's.

11

The statistician can find prize money of $173 in the single event of 1879; compared with $225,000 for all events including the rodeo.

$10 in agricultural grants from the government of the Northwest Territories; $100,000 from the province of Alberta.

Revenue from the first fair will show as nil; from the centennial fair as $5 million — plus $8 million from racing, $4 million from rent of facilities, and a further $4 million from sources like the rodeo and the dining lounges. The lounges alone will bring in $2½ million.

Investment in buildings shows nil for 1879; against 1979 replacement cost of $65 million.

Vehicles parked on the grounds will be no more than a couple of dozen wagons in 1879; 700 thousand motor vehicles a century on.

There were no employees in 1879. A century of progress will show 130 full-time employees and 16 hundred part-time — 300 for the races, 700 in services, and 16 hundred during Klondike Days, the Klondike gold rush being yet another of the major events that helped fill the first hundred years. All together, the equivalent of 775 fulltime jobs where once there were none.

And the volunteers must be counted. One committee put on the fair of 1879; twenty-six supported all activities a century later.

The first committee presumably had six members: the executive plus Captain Gagnon whose help was mentioned in dispatches by Frank Oliver. In 1979 all committees had just about 200 permanent members plus at least that many again during activities.

In 1879 racing days show nil; 156 a century later with $50 million passing through the mutuels. Total purses of zero against $4 million.

Last, but not least, is the amount of cash on hand after the year's operation: $139 following the Fort Edmonton fair, $2 million a century later.

These are figures to which today's volunteer committeemen and employees can point with pride. But when they do they hear no applause from the citizens. They would welcome thunderous applause for what they regard as their achievements, or failing that, polite applause, or failing that, a warm nod of approval. But they seldom win even a frosty nod, and when they compare notes with their counterparts at the Calgary Stampede and the Pacific National Exposition, or any other fair board, they hear the same doleful tale.

The association is not, alas, the only institution to be less popular now than thirty years ago when the writer of this book began reporting city news on radio. The city council, the city police, the Mounted Police, the post office, the armed forces, the oil companies — all have felt admiration turn to antagonism. All blame a bad press, although such a press merely reflects and does not create public opinion. And in recent years the exhibition has been "unfortunate" in some of its publicity. As this was written a large bloc of history was unavailable for reference because it was in police custody. The exhibition people were treating the deprivation with patient good humor, knowing they'd get the records back eventually, but that's much less important than regaining the understanding of the community.

Thirty years ago, and thirty years before that, all parties understood — the public, the shareholders, the government. There was consensus about the exhibition. It was a time and place, a time and place "where City and Country meet." Neat and straightforward, a statement of purpose so absolutely right that it became a slogan without further development. Since then slogan and understanding have been buried in an avalanche of change. City has tripled in size; Country has become much like City; the two have met and sort of all run together. The activities of the association are still those shown on the incorporation certificate of 1908, but, heavens, how the proportions have changed. Obviously the purpose should be redefined and restated. Obviously it hasn't.

To restore mutual understanding, shareholders and public should collaborate on a new declaration of purpose. However, the prospect of useful dialogue between such partners seems less than hopeful. They seem too far apart for discussion except by conference line. A hint of the distance was given at the Coliseum the night the new Northlands logo appeared on the ice. When the house announcer drew attention to the logo the crowd booed. Now, this writer has heard thronging humanity give the Bronx salute to referees, goalkeepers, politicians, pickets, university presidents, theatre managers and the House of Lords but when a crowd boos a logo it tells something about perception.

There are two perceptions of the exhibition association — from within and without, and totally contradictory.

To those inside it seems merely the biggest of service clubs, with volunteers working their hearts out *pro bono publico,* Towards The Public Good as their motto states, volunteers who come in all sizes up to executives of the calibre and daring to bring Edmonton the Coliseum, a hockey palace unsurpassed anywhere.

From the outside, however, the association is often perceived as a private club only slightly less exclusive than the Order of Canada. The Order is limited to 125 living Canadians, the association to 200 living shareholders, with loyalty to neither City nor Country but to a magic kingdom called Northlands, a kingdom with enough horses to supply every Richard III of stage history, a kingdom paying neither rent nor tax, nor heed to public complaints, nor attention to letters from city council requesting information.

These are the parties who must get together to establish a new consensus and understanding. They seem the parties least likely to succeed but who else is there? The search for harmony may well provide even more discord but if there is any consolation in history, the exhibition has never been free of it. Even back in 1879, following the first show at Fort Edmonton, there was controversy.

3 *1880-1890*

The bright promise of that first exhibition day in 1879 proved to be elusive as the packaged nickels in those 5¢ diggers on the midway.

Public support disappeared. So did the treasury. The treasurer died with the $139 surplus in his personal bank account and the widow wouldn't give back the money.

The effort to establish the Exhibition, as a permanent event on a permanent site — was a struggle that went on for many years.

Each step of the way, forwards, backwards and sideways, was chronicled in the Edmonton Bulletin, a paper whose reporting style bore the vigorous imprint of Frank Oliver. The writers were never spectators alone but active participants. To attempt improvement on their eyewitness accounts would be presumptuous, so this phase of the story will be told through excerpts, with here and there an explanatory note. For twenty years and more there was good news and bad news. First the bad news:

December 17 1880

The Edmonton people have suddenly grown indifferent in the matter of agriculture. A little over a year ago the proposal to hold an agricultural show met with the most hearty approval and subscriptions flowed in rapidly. The Secretary Treasurer's statement showed a balance of $139 or thereabouts after paying $160 in prizes. The second annual show was a dismal failure. All the enthusiasm died out and on the appointed day a solitary wagon loaded with produce which could not be excelled in any country was the sole exhibit . . .

. . . . and our great agricultural society goes to smash because not even an officer of the society turns up.

November 5 1881

Our agricultural society, the first ever organized in the Northwest, appears to have gone decidedly dead . . .

It is rather too bad in a new country like this to let an institution of such usefulness fall through, not for lack of funds but merely through lack of interest. There is no doubt that here where new varieties of seeds and animals are so much needed and so hard to get, the society could be worked to the great advantage of the country in general and members of the society in particular.

September 9 1882

Public opinion here is unanimously in favour of holding an agricultural exhibition this year . . . It is a well known fact that the people of the districts to the south and east of us have been making a dead set against Edmonton of late years, filling the ears of intending settlers with the greatest falsehoods in regard to the country. All here are interested in inducing immigration as much as can possibly be done by fair means, and the best way to do this, and at the same time meet the allegations that have been made against our district, is to get the best samples of farm produce we can and send them to other places so that people can judge for themselves.

October 21 1882

The weather on Thursday last was all that could be desired for exhibition purposes . . . Work was suspended in town nearly all day and between 200 and 300 people came in from the surrounding country to see the show. Altogether there were 190 entries. A. Macdonald & Co's new hotel served as an agricultural hall, Donald McLeod's corral held the loose stock; the oxen, pigs and poultry were tied or piled around promiscuously; the horses were pranced up and down the main street in front of the building, the crowd disposed of themselves each as he thought best, and whole affair had a free and easy air refreshingly different from the usual appearance of such affairs in other places where iron clad rule and pugnacious petty authority hold sway. Of course here the managers had not the irrepressible small boy to contend with and therefore they could allow a laxity of rule that, had he been present, in force, would have resulted in chaos.

Entries were in seventeen categories: agricultural horses, native horses, Durham cattle, grade cattle, sheep, pigs, poultry, field grain, field roots and vegetables, preserves, dairy products, home made woollen goods, needlework, leatherwork, and blacksmithing.

(No entries were made in blacksmithing or sheep). This is to be regretted as there are plenty of sheep in the country and in fact one flock was grazing around the exhibition ground all day.

July 7 1883

A meeting of the directors of the Edmonton district agricultural society was held at the school house, Edmonton, on Tuesday July 3. Present: M. McCauley, president, and Messrs. Ross, Stewart, Mulkins and Patton, directors. . . . . Moved by S. D. Mulkins, seconded by A. D. Patton, that the annual exhibition be on Wednesday October 10, 1883. Carried.

..... several of the good qualities of an exhibition were last Wednesday conspicuous by their absence. It is much more likely that the future fame of Edmonton will rest upon its manufactures than upon its agricultural interests, unsurpassed as these are, and any exhibitions of her products which takes no notice of her coal, her iron, her gold, does her scant justice. It is in vain to say that because all these minerals can be mined in paying quantities within half a mile of the town the people must therefore know all about them and there is no use placing them upon exhibition. This is not so. The people are scandalously ignorant on this subject, and doubtless it is within the mark to say that not one half of the people know that any brownish boulder they pick up on the bank of the river is almost certain to be more than a third of it pure iron.

The same public-spirited souls who gave the community an autumn exhibition also provided a program of summer fun on Dominion Day.

In time these events merged to become the summer fair of the current century.

The Bulletin gives a glowing account of the fun on Canada's seventeenth birthday.

July 5 1884

DOMINION DAY

Notwithstanding the inclement weather fully 300 people assembled to witness the sports and games which came off under the auspices of the Edmonton districts sports committee. Quite a number of the fair sex favored the games with their presence in the afternoon. Booths and tents were erected on the grounds where the national beverage of the North-West — hop beer, or as it is more properly designated, "slush" — was dished out to the enthusiastic sports and their friends. The usual amount of "exhilarating liquid" was partaken of by the pink-eye club, without causing the usual results, as with the exception of some "wind fights" nothing of a pugilistic nature marred the day's proceedings.

The principal event of the day was the tug of war between Edmonton and Big Lake (St. Albert). Twelve men were ranged on each side. Edmonton had the advantage of weight and Big Lake that of being used to such work as the team was composed mostly of raftsmen.

The horse races were well contested, especially the half mile dash, but the Edmonton turf has sadly degenerated since the glorious days of the good old horse Rowdy, and the old sports Dan Driscoll and Jim Campbell.

Betting was indulged in to a limited extent. One party is known to have lost all of two dollars.

16

October 11 1884

The weather on the morning of the Exhibition, Thursday, was all that could be desired, but before nine o'clock a light drizzle set in, which continued with but little intermission all day. Of course this put a damper on the show and, no doubt, hindered it from being the unqualified success that it might, could, would, should, and was expected to have been. Still fully 300 people were present, including many ladies, and there were 268 entries for prizes. The stock and hogs were exhibited on Fraser Avenue (98th Street) near Main Street (Jasper Avenue). Main Street, in front of Kelly's hall, was utilized to show the horses, and ropes were stretched on each side to keep the course clear.

The display of grain was very good and competition was keen. For the wheat prizes there were seventeen entries ...

Some excellent specimens of red and white fife were shown and it may be remarked here that whether it is the fault of the seed or the climate, a Philadelphia lawyer could not tell the difference between the two varieties. Although the wheat was good, the barley excelled it and might safely challenge the world to competition. The seed onions were scarcely up to the standard of other years in size but still they were large enough to beat anything raised elsewhere in Canada outside of a hothouse.

January 31 1885

The annual meeting of the Edmonton Agricultural Society was held in the school house, Edmonton, on Monday afternoon, Jan. 26, commencing at 2 p.m. The President, M. McCauley in the chair.

... R. McKernan thought, though himself a director, that the business had been run in rather loose and careless fashion last year.

Men had taken away prize money who were not members of the society until the day of the show, if they were then. He thought tickets should be printed and distributed so that members might be known.

... The president said it had been agreed by the directors that the expense of printing tickets should not be incurred, and that if any person was mean enough to say that he belonged to the society when he did not for the sake of saving 25 cents, he was to be allowed admission.

At the conclusion of the agenda the meeting voted on resolutions concerned not with agriculture but with general government. The society was the only local body with legal status in the political structure of the Northwest Territories.

A school board had been authorized but not yet set up. Edmonton would remain unincorporated and without a town council until 1892. So the agricultural society was the only organization which could give weight to the views of the people. The meeting voted support of four resolutions: that police officers not be allowed to sit as magistrates; that the federal government raise the powers of the Northwest Council to those of a provincial government; that informers no longer get half the fine on conviction of a bootlegger, and that a poundkeeper be appointed.

The spring of 1885 brought concerns which overshadowed poundkeepers and rewards of moonshine informers. For several weeks Edmonton was besieged by Indian supporters of Louis Riel and the disruption of peaceful pursuits was noted among the entries at the fall exhibition.

October 10 1885

The 4th annual exhibition of the present Edmonton agricultural society was held on Tuesday last in A. Macdonald & Co.'s building and on the grounds adjoining.

In . . . roots the show was not up to the mark of previous years, caused to some extent by the troubles of last spring preventing gardening from being indulged in. Some very large cabbage were shown by the Roman Catholic mission, some excellent cauliflower by Mr. Lambert of Fort Saskatchewan, and four large, perfectly ripe melons by W. Anderson, Indian agent.

The leading feature in horses was a fine two year old part Clydesdale stallion of a steel grey color which had just been brought in from Ontario by Mr. A. Adamson.

Jas. Gille exhibited a side of home cured bacon, getting an extra prize, and the remark was general that the hog industry here is assuming such proportions that prizes should be offered for home-cured bacons and hams.

A specimen of pemmican was exhibited and the way in which it was promptly pulled to pieces and devoured, a dog carrying off the parchment in which it was enclosed, was a great reminder of the old times.

October 2 1886

The fifth annual exhibition of the Edmonton Agricultural society will be held on Thursday next. If there was not another agricultural exhibition held in the country it would still be advisable to hold one in Edmonton. This is at present the most northerly purely agricultural settlement on the continent. Consequently farming is to a very great extent experimental. Experiment has proved that some grains and vegetables which a few years ago it was thought impossible to raise here grow well, and that the climate and country are extra well suited for the raising of all the domestic animals. The exhibition gives every man the advantage of the exhibitors' experience instead of having to experiment for himself in each line, thereby increasing the general knowledge at the least individual expense.

September 3 1887

The Calgary Tribune complains that very little interest is taken in the approaching Calgary agricultural exhibit.

September 10 1887

The Toronto industrial exhibition was formally opened by the Governor General on Thursday.

October 3 1887

The Prize List for the Edmonton and St. Albert Agricultural Society's show, which takes place on October 26th, has been issued. The total value of prizes amounts to $600. There is an increase of one dollar on each prize offered for horses, cattle, sheep and hogs over last year's list. Some of the minor prizes are also increased and a class of school exhibits consisting of writing, map drawing and crayon drawing are added.

October 15 1887

The Calgary Tribune's report of the agricultural exhibit in that town which was closed on September 29 says of the exhibits in the agricultural hall scarcely too much could be said in praise . . .

About seventy gentlemen sat down to the society's dinner. A number of very practical speeches were made.

October 29 1887

On Thursday evening of last week the directors of the Edmonton and St. Albert agricultural society and the judges who had awarded the prizes during the day, to the number of thirteen, sat down to an excellent dinner in the Alberta Hotel. (Total cost $10). Before commencing the usual proceedings it was decided that thirteen being an unlucky number it was advisable to make it fourteen by inviting another guest. Geo. S. Long, chairman of the society, occupied the chair. Jas. McDonald . . . had seen all the agricultural exhibitions except the first and could testify to a very marked progress, especially in ladies' work. Parties in rival districts asserted that this was frozen country. It might be so but it had never yet to depend on government charity for seed grain, and some of these districts had.

October 20 1888

A correspondent of the Calgary Herald thinks the agricultural exhibition should not be held earlier than October 20 in order to give farmers a chance to compete with grain which they are not likely to have threshed out before. He alludes to the tendency of the townspeople to "run" the show.

March 2 1889

The regular meeting of the Edmonton Agricultural Society was held Saturday last in the public school house at 2 o'clock.

February 8 1890

The annual meeting of the Edmonton and St. Albert Agricultural Society was held in the public school house, Edmonton, on Saturday last 2 p.m.

Meet the author: Frank Oliver is the name, a name to contend with in western history. Frank made history at the highest level of government, and wrote it week by week in his pioneer newspaper, the Edmonton Bulletin. Even when Frank got too busy to write it all himself his crunchy personality influenced the work of others.

1891- 95

The nineties brought significant advance. In 1891 the railroad builders moved northward from Calgary to bring the iron horse to South Edmonton, reducing the journey from five days by stagecoach to eighteen hours. In 1892 Edmonton petitioned the government of the Northwest Territories for a municipal corporation. Matt McCauley, vice-president of the agricultural society, was elected mayor, and a greater degree of dignity prevailed in the conduct of all institutions, including the exhibition.

October 31 1892

A meeting of directors of the agricultural society was held at C. Young's office on Saturday afternoon to settle all complaints made about the exhibition. J. F. Adamson pointed out that W. H. Stephens had shown two samples of the same kind of grain and had taken first and second prizes for same. The directors decided that in future such would not be allowed. W. H. Stephens complained that J. C. C. Bremner had shown horses in the ring without ropes, which is against the rules. Bremner acknowledged having done so without knowing of the rules. The points and prizes for the horses so shown were deducted from his prize list. There was also a complaint that he had shown a horse that did not belong to him; this was thoroughly explained and the directors were satisfied the horse did belong to Bremner. J. C. C. Bremner complained that W. H. Stephens had shown some pigs that did not belong to him, it was said that the pigs belonged, at the show time, to C. Gallagher. C. D. T. Becher gave evidence to the effect he heard Gallagher tell several people that the pigs shown by Stephens were his (Gallagher's). This case was postponed on account of Mr. Gallagher being out of town.

December 19 1892

A meeting of directors was held in the secretary's office on Saturday afternoon. Present: president M. McCauley, directors C. Long, J.F. Adamson, R. Kelly, W. Stephens and J. Looby. Gallagher's statement re pigs shown by Stephens was read, and it proved to the satisfaction of the directors that Stephens did own the pigs at the time of the exhibition.

January 30 1893

The adjourned annual meeting of the Edmonton agricultural society was held in Robertson's Hall, on Saturday afternoon at 2 p.m. It was agreed to have a show of stallions, bulls and grain in the spring not later than April 25.

April 13 1893

The date of the stallion and bull show has not been definitely fixed yet as the river may be a little late breaking up this season and it is not desirable to hold the show until the ferries are running.

April 17 1893

Notwithstanding the state of the river the stallion show will come off on the 20th as announced.

April 27 1893

Don't forget the stallion show on Saturday on the race course. Positively no postponement this time.

May 1 1893

The first spring show of the Edmonton agricultural society was held on Saturday afternoon at the race track. The exhibit of horses was excellent in numbers and quality, representing a large investment of capital. It is to be regretted that the offer of prizes for a show of bulls had no effect, not one being brought out.

When the roadster prizes were awarded a procession of horses shown was formed and paraded from the show down Jasper Avenue to the hotel stables.

June 29 1893

Agricultural Society

A meeting of the above society will be held in W. Fielding's warehouse on Saturday, July 8 at 3 p.m. re sending at exhibit to Winnipeg exhibition.

July 20 1893

It has finally been decided that beer should not be sold on the Winnipeg exhibition grounds . . .

August 14 1893

A meeting of the agricultural society of which the mayor (Matt McCauley) is president, is to be held at his office Thursday next to arrange about the forwarding of a car of exhibits to the east, and discuss the sending of two delegates with it.

ere is the scene of the action, any vigorous competitive action of the 1880s and 90s. The sport
ound was on the Hudson's Bay Reserve, on the northwest fringe of the settlement beginning about
2nd Avenue and 103rd Street. There was room for any activity — football, baseball, lacrosse,
icket, footracing, horseracing and events of the fair.

September 11 1893

The firm stand taken by the Edmonton Agricultural Society and
their determination not to send any exhibits at all, unless the CPR
put forward a car direct to Edmonton as they agreed to do, meets
with the hearty approval of both the Fort Saskatchewan and Saint
Albert agricultural societies . . . .

September 14 1893

At last our exhibit is ready for shipment and will go forward in a
box car Friday, which the CPR have at length favored us with. The
delegates accompanying the exhibit are: Geo. Long, Edmonton, J.
Porte, Fort Saskatchewan, and Adolph Meunier, St. Albert. The
wheat, oats and barley which form the cereal part of the exhibit have
mostly been obtained around the Sturgeon River settlement,
(Namao), Clover Bar, St. Albert and Stony Plain.

September 29 1893
Mr. Editor:

Sir: We arrived in Ottawa September 24 and on the 25 our samples were moved to the exhibition grounds by the CPR where they had a space 15 feet long, 6 feet wide and 12 feet high reserved for us. We had thousands of people visit us during the week. They were delighted with our samples and hundreds of them asked if they were not grown on some experimental farm. They thought it impossible for such crops to be grown by every farmer of Fort Saskatchewan and Edmonton.

Yours truly   J. L. Porte

October 2 1893
Round trip tickets to Edmonton will be sold in Calgary at single on Monday, October 9th, good until Friday, October 13th, the object being to give the people of the south country an opportunity to witness the greatest agricultural show on earth — to wit, the Edmonton exhibition.

October 2 1893
A meeting of the directors of the Edmonton agricultural society was held in M. McCauley's office on Saturday. It was decided to hold the show of grain and vegetables in Robertson's Hall and of livestock in the vacant spot east of McCauley's stable.

January 29 1894
The annual meeting of the Edmonton Agricultural Society was held in the town hall on Saturday 27th instant, about 12 members being present. The secretary treasurer read a statement of the affairs of the society for the current year, showing a deficit of some 50 dollars owing to the reduction made in the government grant which it had been assumed would be the same as last year.

June 25 1894
A meeting of the directors of the Edmonton district agricultural society was held in the council chamber on Saturday afternoon to consider the advisability of holding a midsummer show. It was unanimously agreed that the fall of the year was the best time . . . and the date was fixed for Tuesday and Wednesday 9th and 10th of October.

September 27 1894
A ripe pumpkin weighing 37 pounds and measuring 4 feet 5 inches in circumference was grown this summer at Beaver Lake by Robert Logan, and is being used in the culinary department of the Alberta Hotel. Mr. Logan has others much larger that he is keeping to exhibit at the fall fair.

October 4 1894

Four prizes will be given for horse racing at the exhibition on Tuesday and Wednesday next. A purse of $20 is offered for the one mile stallion trot; a purse of $15 for the half mile running race; a purse of $15 for the one mile open trot; and $10 for the quarter mile running race 14½ hands high and under. Three heats will be run in each race.

October 11 1894

Lord Aberdeen, Governor General of Canada and Lady Aberdeen have signified through their private secretary that they will visit Edmonton on Saturday. A special meeting of the town council was held last night when it was arranged that their excellencies would be honoured at a public reception in Robertson Hall on Saturday night when addresses from the town, the agricultural society and the St. Andrews' Society will be presented. Their Excellencies will be met at the station (south side) by Mayor McCauley and driven to the brow of the hill when a torchlight procession headed by the citizens band will conduct them to the hall.

January 3 1895

The ball given in South Edmonton on New Years night by the agricultural society was a grand success. About forty couples danced to the strains furnished by some of the Edmonton orchestra.

January 21 1895

The annual meeting of the Edmonton Agricultural Society was held on Saturday afternoon last in the town council chamber, vice-president McCauley in the chair. About 20 members were present.

The financial statement was read, stating that a deficit of $90 which existed last year, had been reduced to $17.31.

On motion of McCauley and McDiarmid, the disputed award of prizes to creamery butter, in competition with dairy butter, was sustained.

April 4 1895

Cheap rates are being offered to Regina during the Territorial Exhibition — $15.70 good for round trip and to extend one week after fair is over.

May 27 1895

This (24th of May) celebration was the first occasion on which an admission fee to the race grounds in Edmonton was charged. Although the races could be seen very nearly as well from outside the fence as inside, and the fence itself could be passed through almost anywhere, nearly everybody paid the admission fee.

The Governor of General of Canada, Lord Aberdeen, travels to Regina to open the Territorial Exhibition of 1895. Here he meets the Indian chiefs.

July 1 1895

A poster announcing the Territorial Exhibition declares that every Canadian should attend because it is a Canadian enterprise. It may be remarked that the poster is printed in Cincinnati. A peculiar way of encouraging Canadian industry and enterprise.

July 22 1895

In other column we publish the dates for the holding of the first Territorial Exhibition at Regina, the capital of the provisional districts of Alberta, Saskatchewan, and Assinaboia, and from the untiring industry manifested by Lieut. Governor Mackintosh and the hearty response accorded the enterprise by the various agricultural societies and leading men generally, the enterprise should be crowned with complete success.

Many would have preferred an autumn exhibition, but that became an impossibility, in consequence of railway rolling stock being busy at that time, conveying livestock to the large eastern exhibitions. To get very low rates for travel and free transport for bona fide exhibits, Manitoba was obliged to adopt a summer date and Lieut. Governor Mackintosh had no other recourse than do likewise.

Regina, July 25 1895

The Territorial Exhibition opened today and is a phenomenal success. There were over 6,000 entries on Saturday and they are still coming. The entries include 700 head of stock. The minister of the interior arrived this morning.

Here he opens the Exhibit Hall, from which a banner flaunts the proud names of the three Provisional Districts: Assiniboia, Alberta and Saskatchewan.

September 16 1895
Fall Fairs

Lacombe Agricultural Society, September 26; Fort Saskatchewan Agricultural Society, October 2; Beaver Lake Agricultural Society, October 5; Edmonton Agricultural Society, October 4 and 5; South Edmonton Agricultural Society, October 7

October 7 1895

The fall show of the Edmonton agricultural society which was held on Friday and Saturday was highly favoured as to weather, but the number of exhibits in almost all the important classes was smaller than usual. The principal exception was in horses, and especially in young horses, which showed up in larger numbers than ever, of excellent quality, showing that this is a good country in which to raise horses . . . .

W. T. Henry & Co. occupied an ample space with a display of gents' furnishings which would have done credit to a city.

C. Gallagher had a show case in which were arranged samples of prepared meats such as spiced roll, sausages, bologna, head cheese, roll bacon, etc. Jas. Dale displayed a number of the styles of the Singer sewing machine to great advantage.

5 1896-1900

At this point the Edmonton Exhibition disappears abruptly from the news. From 1896 through 1900 one reads about fairs east, west, south and north, but not here. A disappearance mysterious, total and unexplained has put Edmonton's fair in the same oblivion as the lost continent of Atlantis.

How could anything so big and so noisy as an exhibition vanish without trace? There must be a clue somewhere. And there is, if you look sharply at the Bulletin of January 24 1895:

Board of Trade Meeting
Mr. Woodsworth suggests that action be taken by the Board to assist the Agricultural Society in procuring grounds and erecting buildings with a view to establishing an agricultural exhibition for northern Alberta, instead of merely a local exhibition as at present.

So that solves the mystery. The fair sank from sight not from lack of support but the very opposite, to rise again bigger and better, a rival for Calgary's show — the Inter-Western Pacific Exposition.

The board of trade was years pondering locations — there were so many to choose from. In the meantime the Bulletin was obliged to report progress of fairs in other centres of population, including South Edmonton, the upstart rival town across the river. Though not yet incorporated as Strathcona, the town's agricultural society owned a fine site, bordered on the north by University Avenue and the east by 104th Street, a site which became the fabled South Side Athletic Grounds and is still a centre of sport. In Edmonton's "no fair" season the Bulletin reported with obvious pique:

October 1 1896
The annual exhibition of the South Edmonton agricultural society was held on Tuesday and Wednesday at the show grounds. The roadway from the town ... and the roads inside ... will no doubt be improved before next year's show and prove what can really be done in roadmaking in this district. The programme stated that judging would start at 12 o'clock, but it was two o'clock before they got to work.

The ladies of the Presbyterian church had a luncheon booth on the grounds which was well patronized.

October 5 1896

The annual fall fair of the Fort Saskatchewan agricultural society was held on Friday and Saturday last, and was favored with fine weather although a little raw for standing around. Everything passed off without a hitch; the best of order prevailing throughout. The ladies of the Presbyterian church supplied dinner and also had a booth on the grounds which was well patronized.

October 15 1896

The third annual fall fair of the Lacombe agricultural society was held on the 6th and was a pronounced success. The great interest taken in the fair and the increasing number of exhibits will necessitate enlarged buildings soon.

December 21 1896

Fort Saskatchewan: The agricultural society ball was held on the 16th in the town hall and in point of attendance was a grand success, and as the immediate object was to raise funds for the fall show, this was an important and pleasing feature. Great interest was taken in a voting contest over a cake.

Your correspondent failed to find out what the voting was really about. Whether voting on who took the cake or cut it, or how many rings was embedded in it, was a puzzle; but as the financial result nets the society a goodly sum it matters little.

December 28 1896

South Edmonton agricultural society's ball will be on New Year's Eve.

July 22 1897

Fort Saskatchewan: The agricultural society's new grounds (22 acres recently granted by the federal government) were the scene of great activity on Saturday last. A "Bee" had been organized for clearing off the brush on the centre of the track grounds, and some 40 of the settlers turned out and worked like beavers and completed in a short space of time the work they had undertaken. In addition to the men there were seven teams, working scrapers and a grader on the track itself. If every settlement had the same kind of enterprising people, it would brighten up the different districts immensely.

September 30 1897

The fourth fall exhibition of South Edmonton agricultural society was held on Tuesday and Wednesday in the spacious grounds of the society south of the town. The grounds are twenty acres in extent surrounded by a high board fence. A good half mile race track has been laid out and improved, a grandstand built and everything done to put the shows of the agricultural society on a permanent footing. A small agricultural hall has been built within the grounds for the display of agricultural and dairy products, fancy work etc.

August 11 1898

Fort Saskatchewan: The working members of the agricultural society started the fence around the agricultural grounds here on Saturday and got about half done. They are busy at it today again and will finish tonight. The farmers in the surrounding area deserve a great deal of credit for the way in which they turn out to do work of this kind.

We hope to see a good turn out of Edmonton people to see our small race meet.

September 29 1898

F. Oliver went to Lacombe on Tuesday's train to attend the opening of the new hall of the Lacombe agricultural society.

October 13 1898

Lacombe Fair — The exhibition on the 7th and 8th proved to be very successful both as to exhibits and attendance. Several visitors were present from Calgary, Red Deer and Wetaskiwin besides the surrounding country. The new hall is just what is needed and as the society has purchased quite large grounds there is ample space for a good display of livestock. The vegetables, as usual, were typical of Alberta, prodigious in size and quite a sight to an eastern native. A number of fine prizes were given, testifying to the liberality of the people and the prosperity of Alberta.

December 19 1898

Annual ball of the South Edmonton Agricultural Society on Friday, December 30th.

February 16 1899

South Edmonton Agricultural Society. In accordance with a resolution passed at the last meeting of the above society, a meeting will be held in Ross's Hall, South Edmonton, on Saturday March 4 at 2 o'clock p.m. to discuss means to encourage capitalists and manufacturers to locate in this district.

July 6 1899

Wetaskiwin's annual celebration takes place this month. The exact date has not been decided on. Five hundred dollars in prizes will be given and events will consist of horse racing, bicycle racing, athletic sports and Indian tea dance, all to wind up with a display of fireworks in the evening.

By this time the south side rival was formally incorporated as the town of Strathcona and in July this proud advertisement went forth:

Northern Alberta's
Great Industrial Fair

By the South Edmonton Agricultural Society

TUESDAY AND WEDNESDAY

July 25th & 26th, 1899

—AT—

STRATHCONA.

The first Summer Fair held in Northern Alberta.

$1,500 IN PRIZES.

Exhibits of Horses, Cattle and other Live Stock, Poultry, Grain, Farm Produce, Ladies' Work, Art Exhibits, Etc.

Baseball Match--Edmonton vs. Strathcona--at 10 a. m., July 26th.

PROGRAMME OF RACES :

FIRST DAY.

		1st	2nd	3rd
1	Named Race, one mile, 3 in 5. Purse $50	$25	$15	8
	(Blackthorn, Ollie M., Ontario Volunteer, Jimmy Mitchell.)			
2	Farmers' Trot or Pace, green, 1 mile, 2 in 3. Purse $30	$15	10	5
3	Open Run, 1 mile, 2 in 3. Purse $50	$25	15	5

SECOND DAY

		1st	2nd	3rd
4	Open Trot or Pace, 1 mile, 3 in 5. Purse $100	$50	35	15
5	Open Run, half mile, 2 in 3. Purse $35	$20	10	
6	Three Minute Race, 1 mile, 3 in 5. Purse $50	$25	15	10
7	Pony Race, half mile, 2 in 3. Purse $15	$8	5	2
8	Indian Red River Cart Race, ½ mile dash. 1st 100lb. sack flour	2nd 50lb sack		

Entrance for Races No. 1, 3, 4, 5 and 6 must be made not later than 9 o'clock p. m. before the first day of Fair. Four to enter and three to start. Any horse distancing the field, entitled to first money only. Entry fee 10 per cent of purse. American Association Rules to govern. Horses eligible from date of bill.

ADMISSION TO GROUNDS, 25c.

Jas. McKernan, Pres.   H. Wilson, Sec'y

Strathcona, June 29th, 1899.

Arrangements have been made with the C. P. R. to run excursions from eastern points to meet this Exhibition, leaving eastern points July 13th and 18th, good for two months. Round trip $40.00

August 24 1899

The prize lists for the Fort Saskatchewan exhibition are out. It is to be held Friday, September 29. Competition is open to the Northwest Territories and everybody is invited. The prize list is liberal and well arranged. As the centre of a large and progressive farming district, the fair at Fort Saskatchewan should be a success.

August 28 1899

The Interwestern Pacific Exhibition will be held in Calgary September 27 and 28. Prizes to the amount of $3,000 will be offered. Special railway rates have been secured. This fair is the beginning of what is hoped will become the great fair of the western part of Central Canada as the Winnipeg fair is of the eastern part. All information on application to John De Sousa, secretary.

August 31 1899

The Toronto exhibition has been formally opened.

August 31 1899

The first of the monthly fairs to be held by the settlers of Stony Plain and Spruce Grove will be held Monday next, the 4th September at the Spruce Grove Store . .

October 5 1899

Coal for Paris Exposition

W. W. Scott, sub commissioner for the Canadian exhibit at the Paris exhibition hints that he would like to secure a block of Edmonton coal a foot square. Miners able to supply this should communicate with Mr. Scott at Ottawa at once . . .

January 8 1900

It was decided to hold a summer fair at Strathcona on the 1st and 2nd of August next. The secretary treasurer read a statement showing that the grounds purchased by the association for exhibition purposes have been paid for in full, and the association now has on hand cash and assets. $1,100.

March 23 1900

Fort Saskatchewan: The agricultural ball held here on March 21 was a success both socially and financially, the proceeds amounting to $95. In the voting contest for the most popular young lady, Miss Graham was elected by a 115 majority and was presented with a gold watch.

July 16 1900

Winnipeg Exhibition: Instructions have been received by Stationmaster English to sell tickets for the Winnipeg exhibition on the 18th, 20th and 21st, next Wednesday, Friday and Saturday. No instructions as to the price of tickets have been received, but it is supposed the fare will be the same as last year, $22 for round trip.

July 25 1900

Citizen's day at the Winnipeg fair resulted in an estimated attendance of 30,000 people. Judging is completed in many classes. The fair is a great success. Thousands of Americans are here.

August 3 1900

The Strathcona Summer Fair took place on Wednesday and Thursday last and was successful beyond expectation. . . . . The Strathcona Agricultural Society are to be congratulated on the success of their experiment of a summer fair. The event has proven that while a summer fair has its drawbacks it also has its advantages, an important one being that a date can be fixed on which farmers can have the necessary leisure in which to take an active interest in the fair's progress. The great interest of a fall fair is its being a comparison of the crowning result of the season of growth. But against that is the fact that in the Northwest farmers are generally very busy at that season . . .

August 6 1900

Balloon Ascension

The balloon ascension on Wednesday afternoon from the Strathcona fair grounds was very successful and brought out strong expressions of approval from all who witnessed it. The balloon, which was inflated with hot air, rose rapidly almost straight up from its moorings. Professor Thompson did a number of acrobatic feats from the trapeze, while the balloon was ascending. When a height had been reached at which he looked like a very small boy he made the descent safely with a parachute. When the balloon had been relieved of his weight, it tilted to one side, allowing the air to escape. Very soon the balloon reversed and as the hot air was forced out by the descent the balloon was soon empty and came down just outside the fair grounds like a dish rag.

6 1899-1900

Meanwhile, back across the river in Edmonton, where exhibition spirit had done its own imitation of a wet dishrag, there came a renaissance. You'll recall the board of trade committee which set out, in 1895, on an expedition to locate a site for a permanent fair. This band of adventurers worked so quietly there was no news of it for years. But finally, into the bleak February void of 1899, burst word that came like certain news to Queen Isabella of Spain in 1492. The committee had discovered land.

February 2 1899

The committee appointed by the board of trade to secure offers for exhibition grounds . . . . have decided to accept that of the H.B. Co., of 55 acres on the flat immediately in front of town. The property is bounded on the south by the river, on the east by the estate of Donald Ross (101 Street), on the north by Calgary Avenue (96 Avenue), and on the west Fourth Street, the street which is graded to a winter crossing of the river. The price is $7,000; $500 down and the balance in nine annual instalments with interest at 7 percent.

February 23 1899

A largely attended meeting was held in Robertson Hall on Tuesday evening to form an agricultural association and acquire suitable land for a public park and race track.

A society called "The Edmonton Industrial Association" was formed and the following were appointed provisional directors: John A. McDougall, Thos. Bellamy, Wm. Short, J. H. Morris, E. C. Emery, C. Gallagher, G. R. Kirkpatrick, S. Lane, and W. S. Robertson. Mr. Emery was also appointed secretary-treasurer of the association.

The directors propose to improve the site selected by fencing it and building a race track, and will also probably hold an agricultural show. The capital stock of the association will be $20,000, of which $11,000 has been subscribed.

February 27 1899

The meeting called for Tuesday the 28th at 8 pm for subscribers to the exhibition association has been postponed until further notice.

June 29 1899

The grading of the race track was finished yesterday by S. F. McCauley, who had the contract and who has carried it out most successfully. The course itself is much better than the old one ever was and has been levelled, graded and rolled into excellent condition. The old grandstand has been moved down and set upon the grounds, the fencing will be completed today and everything will be in readiness by Saturday. Dancing and refreshment booths are springing up all over the grounds. The sod has been removed from the baseball diamond, but the dogwood outside is liable to bother the fielders considerably.

June 29 1899

Owing to the lack of a proper track to practice on and also on account of the wet weather which has been unfavorable to wheeling, it is doubtful if the bicycle club will be able to arrange a programme of races for July 1st here.

July 3 1899

The reputation enjoyed by Edmonton of always having a good celebration when it had any, was sufficient to bring one of the largest crowds ever gathered here to witness the sports on Dominion Day, on the new grounds of the Industrial Exhibition Association. It is estimated that between three and four thousand people were on the grounds.

The weather was delightful and the program of athletic and racing events was carried through without a hitch and without an unpleasant incident.

At 9:30 A.M. the procession composed of the band, citizens and Indians rode Main Street, the latter being in large numbers and riding with precision almost military. At the grounds the scene was a busy one, full of life and color.

July 3 1899

The visiting Indians are parading the streets today and favoring the public with vocal and instrumental selections.

HONOR ROLL of Petitioners

Cornelius Gallagher *pork packer*
John Alexander McDougall *merchant*
Thomas Bellamy *merchant*
Stanislaus LaRue *merchant*
Walter Scott Robertson *deputy sheriff*
Joseph Henry Morris *merchant*
George Robert Foster Kirkpatrick *banker*
William Short *advocate*
Edward Corrigan Emery *advocate*
George Thomas Bragg *agent*
George Johnston Kinnaird *town clerk*
Issaac Cowie *agent*
Frank Fraser Tims *agent*
John Edward Graham *clerk*
Herbert Aldridge *clerk*
Frank Osborne *collector of customs*
Abraham Cristall *merchant*
Joseph Hormidas Gariepy *merchant*
George Bellamy *merchant*
Phillip Umbach *clerk*
Reinhold Matz *hotelkeeper*
Henry William Moller *hotelkeeper*
John Looby *harness maker*
John Spratt Willmott *banker*
James Lorenzo Johnson *merchant*
Joseph Eugene Laurencelle *bank manager*
Louis Joseph Cartier *bank accountant*
William Thomas Henry *merchant*
Harry Havelock Robertson *advocate*
John Bryon Mercer *merchant*
Neville White *gentleman*
St. George Jellett *general agent*
Kenneth Wellington McKenzie *merchant*
Emmanuel Raymer *jeweler*
Donald Walter McDonald *druggist*
James Thomas Blowey *furniture dealer*
William Johnstone Walker *merchant*
Hedley Clarence Taylor *advocate*
Alex Taylor *postmaster*
Henry Astley *merchant*
Walter Bethune Stennett *fur buyer*
John Norris *rancher*
Philippe Roy *physician*
William Herring Cooper *clerk*
Thomas Gifford Hutchings *merchant*
James Ross *merchant*
Donald Ross *gardener*
Frederick Ross *merchant*
Robert Hockley *barber*
Albert Edward Potter *auctioneer*
John Kennedy *farmer*
Nicholas D. Beck *advocate*
James Gibbon *Indian agent*
William Harold Clark *contractor*
Matthew M. McCauley *proprietor cartage company*
Thomas W. Lines *grain dealer*
Joseph Chenier *merchant*
John Allan McPherson *farmer Spruce Grove*
James McDiarmid *farmer Poplar Lake*

George Hutton *farmer*
Arthur Gregory Harrison *civil engineer*
Thomas Wellington Chalmers *dominion land surveyor*
Joseph Henri Picard *merchant*
Richard Secord *merchant*
Frank Oliver *journalist*
Samuel Fear McCauley *contractor*
Samuel Nankin *jeweler*
H. Sigler *general merchant*
Georges Roy *registrar*
Peter G. Campbell *drayman*
P. Edmond Lessard *accountant*
Daniel Brox *farmer Spruce Grove*
John Owens *horse dealer Calgary*
Duncan C. Robertson *contractor*
Thomas A. Gregg *newspaperman*
Henry G. Silver *merchant*
William Ford Langworthy *rancher*
F. E. Moroney *accountant*
Joseph William Kelly *store manager*
Thomas Hourston *fur buyer*
Alfred Hutchings *farmer*
Richard McIntosh *merchant*
Joseph Whitelaw *merchant*
L. J. Ostrander *agent*
N. B. Peek *agent*
J. H. Sheddon *agent*
Charles Henry Hubbell *accountant*
John Darley Harrison *physician*
Robert Logan *rancher*
Thomas G. Lauder *clerk*
William Richardson *agent*
James J. Dunlop *accountant*
James A. Stovel *merchant*
R. J. Manson *contractor*
John H. Montgomery *merchant*
Ferdinand Mayerhoffer *dyeman*
Joseph Hostyn *hotel clerk*
Arthur William Ormsby *electrical engineer*
Henri Morel *contractor*
Alexis F. Degagne *contractor*
Joseph Larose and Sterratt
Edward Looby *blacksmith*
Alexander Fraser *contractor*
Henry Hetu *hotelkeeper*
David J. Collins *harnessmaker*
Wing Lee *laundryman*
William Storie *farmer*
Henry Goodridge *agent*
Frederic Villeneuve *advocate*
Godfrid Corriveau *mechanic*
Joseph N. Pomerleau *contractor*
Henry Allen Gray *Clerk in Holy Orders*
Gilbert Berg *baker*
Leslie F. Price *painter*
Axell G. Engstrom *painter*
James Tough *farmer*
Edmond Brosseau *merchant St. Albert*

On this fateful July third, however, a number of prominent people were too busy for concerts. The sports had been a gratifying success. More important, the location had proved a winner. In the affairs of men there comes a time for many things. This was a time to buy. In his office of law, E. C. Emery drew up the documents by which Con Gallagher and John A. McDougall bought the site as trustees for an association to be incorporated as quickly as possible. The price was still $7,000 — $500 down and the balance over ten years. This done, Mr. Emery addressed himself to composing another legal document — a petition for Territorial authorities in Regina — defining the aims and aspirations of Gallagher, McDougall and like-minded citizens.

The petition would be accompanied on its journey to Regina by a massive list of signatures — of men prepared to subscribe twenty-five dollars each with an immediate call of ten percent.

The petition was duly advertised, which meant three exposures in the Bulletin, on July 16, 23 and 30, 1899: . . . The purposes for which incorporation is sought are: To exhibit and receive for exhibition, permanently or periodically, in structures, buildings or enclosures, in any place or places at or near the Town of Edmonton, in the District of Alberta, N.W.T., any and every variety of thing and being found in animal or vegetable life, and any and every mineral product; to exhibit and receive for exhibition any and all goods, wares, merchandise, machinery, mechanical inventions, and improvements, and works of art of every kind and description, and industrial, agricultural, horticultural, mineral or other products, either manufactured or grown, or in the process of manufacture or growth, and such other products and things as are generally exhibited at fairs or industrial or other exhibitions; to conduct and hold horse and bicycle races and race meetings of every kind; to conduct and hold athletic sports and games of every description; to encourage the improvement of agriculture in all its parts and branches; to award and pay the exhibitor or contestant in any exhibition, race, game, or sport, such prizes, medals or honorary distinctions as may be deemed proper and expedient, to let, lease, and own stalls, stands, rooms and places, in any of its buildings and structures, or on any part of its property, upon such terms and conditions as to the said company shall seem best; and generally to do all such acts, matters, deeds and things necessary or incidental to the holding and conducting of industrial exhibitions, race meetings, athletic games and sports . . . .

Support was pledged by 117 citizens, for whom Edmonton was not merely a town but a cause, a cause to be advanced by public display whenever opportunity knocked. Their names and occupations appeared three times with publication of the petition. The list is an undoubted honor roll of pioneer believers, and is shown in that style on the opposite page.

On August 21 1899 the Edmonton Industrial Exhibition Association was incorporated by a grant of Letters Patent, and early the next year began figuring in the news.

March 9 1900
Board of Trade Meeting

On motion of Bellamy — Gallagher the secretary was instructed to write the departments of agriculture at Ottawa and Regina, informing them of the existence and objects of the Edmonton Industrial Exhibition association and asking grants in aid of the association, mentioning that the Edmonton Agricultural Society has long been dormant and of no use.

June 9 1900

A meeting of the shareholders of the Industrial Exhibition Association will be held tonight at 8 o'clock in the council chamber for the transaction of important business.

June 15 1900
Edmonton's Big Day

The celebration of Dominion Day here on the 2nd and 3rd promises to exceed anything of the kind ever before held in Edmonton. All that is needed to ensure the success that is anticipated is fair weather — with a temporary cessation of those warm and soaking showers which are causing such luxuriant growth.

The idea is to have the sports the best the country can produce and the celebration the biggest the town can hold.

Arrangements are being made by the committee to add to the attractions on both days a broncho busting and roughriding exhibition by Messrs. Austin and Lumas from Texas.

July 13 1900
Town Council

A letter from the secretary of the Board of Trade was read asking that the council make a grant to meet the expenses of the party taking charge of the Edmonton district exhibit at the Winnipeg exhibition, ... The unanimous desire of the council that the exhibit be made the best the district could produce finally embodied in the motion granting $100, twenty five of which is to go to furnishing literature descriptive of Northern Alberta.

August 24 1900

After an intermission of several years the Edmonton fall fair is to be resumed. As far as the season is concerned, we frequently have the finest weather of the year in October and November ... At a general meeting of the company held July 9th, the provisional directors were elected a board of management. In order that a clear idea of what would best meet the conditions of the country ... should be arrived at, authority was given to add to the board well-known farmers from several parts of the district.

August 31 1900

The Industrial Exhibition association are calling for tenders for the erection of an agricultural building on the grounds.

September 21 1900

The directors have called off the exhibition which was announced for October 23rd, 24th and 25th, it being thought the lateness of the harvest would prevent a large attendance.

January 24 1901

At a meeting of the directors of the Industrial Exhibition association on Monday, it was decided to hold the annual meeting on the 20th of February in Robertson Hall at 8 pm to receive report of provisional directors and elect officers for the ensuing year, and particularly to discuss arrangements for holding a summer fair.

A turn of the page will reveal what the boosters have wrought. A summer morning sun lights the scene for C. W. Mathers, who has set his camera on Saskatchewan Drive, a few blocks east of the point from which George Mercer Dawson photographed the fairground of 1879. Mathers shoots over top of Ochsner's brewery, replaced later by the Northwest brewery, parts of which remain as a museum. Nearest object on the north bank is the first municipal power plant. Beyond are the exhibition race track, the woods in which fair patrons park their horses in shade, and Ottewell's feed mill, on the track of the Edmonton Yukon and Pacific Railway. Donald Ross' Edmonton Hotel still welcomes travellers at the foot of McDougall Hill. Up above, two spires on the skyline are the second McDougall Church and the Edmonton Public School.

(293) EDMONTON
B 9985

7 The Big Fair

April 19 1901

"Old Timers Day" promises to be the event of the July celebrations here. A pageant thoroughly representative of the old time life conditions is being arranged, with bands of Indians in gala attire, Red River carts, cayuses, cowboys and many other features peculiar to the west, especially in its earlier and more romantic days. On the grounds the canvas villages of the Crees and Stoneys will spring up and the land that was once the Indians' will be theirs again for a day and a night. Indian and half breed races will be held and to the hum of the tuneful tom tom, Indian dances will be given in all their barbaric magnificence.

April 29 1901

Big Fair Directors Meet.

The directors of the Industrial Exhibition met on Saturday evening in the secretary's office, all the directors being present. The contracts were awarded for the building of the grandstand and exhibition buildings.

May 10 1901

Calgary's fair July 10th to 13th

Estimates of the prize list committee were passed at a meeting of the Calgary sports committee held last week. They provided altogether for the handsome sum of $10,000 for prizes and attractions for the coming exhibition. This amount is considerably in advance of last year which was only $6,000. The special feature of the exhibition will be the livestock, it will be above all a western stock show. Large prizes will be offered for all kinds of cattle and horses, and particularly for military remounts.

May 13 1901

The Big Fair

Contractors McLeod and Dietz are busy hauling lumber to their respective building sites. Mr. McLeod, who has the contract for the exhibition building, will erect his structure on the east side of the track. Mr. Dietz, who is building the grandstand, is also erecting it on the east side, opposite the one already up.

The committee of management have about closed the contract with the Red River theatrical circuit for the outdoor attractions, which will be on the same lines as those shown at Winnipeg, Brandon, and Fargo. The committee expects the attractions will include balloon ascensions, tight rope walking, acrobatics and contortionists.

May 27 1901

A handsome gold medal will be presented by the Edmonton Industrial Association to the merchant having the best decorated store during fair week. A beautiful silver medal will be offered for the best decorated dwelling during the fair. All citizens are asked by the association to decorate their homes in order to beautify the town.

May 31 1901

The prize list of the Industrial Exhibition association for the summer fair here in July have now been issued by the Bulletin. The lists contain 76 pages.

June 7 1901

Things are booming on the fair grounds . . . . The building and grounds committee have laid out the site for the new stables and also the pens for sheep, cattle and swine and construction work has commenced on them.

The Northwest government has undertaken to furnish expert judges for livestock, sending them to Edmonton at their own expense. The directors are very much pleased at the action of the government as this will ensure fair competition and no favor to anyone.

June 7 1901
Preparing for the Fair

Improvements continue apace on the exhibition grounds. A little Village is springing up among the trees and the scene around the track is a busy one. A large number of men with teams and scrapers are at work grading and widening the track. The course will be graded so it will drain itself and so dry quickly. Twenty-five feet is being added to its width, the work being in charge of S. F. McCauley. For the accommodation of race horses the association is having built some 25 stalls where they may be cared for. Construction starts today. In addition there will be 150 cattle pens for use of exhibitors of livestock. Twelve men are out today cutting out the underbrush from among the trees north of the track. . . . The track proper is being fenced on the inside and outside, and rigs will not be allowed across the course or on the green inside. This green will be converted into a football, baseball, lacrosse and cricket ground. An attraction platform 50 by 35 feet . . . is being built directly in front of the grandstand, across the track.

June 7 1901

The program of platform attractions at the July fair has been forwarded by the Minneapolis Attraction Company. Each of the attraction will perform twice a day, making in all twelve performances each day. The different "turns" will be: The Richards Family, three in number, aerial artists, combining revolving ladder and Japanese pole acts. The turn runs from 20 to 25 minutes. The De Vallas, three in number. A very funny turn introducing a horizontal bar act.

Professor Bell, a Japanese slack wire and juggling act. Prof. Bell juggles every conceivable object from a cigarette paper to knives, cigar boxes etc. Professor Norquist, high diver. From a jumping pole Prof. Norquist jumps into a net from a height of 65 feet.

Mathews and Newman, unicycle and rolling globe acts. Prof. C. Richards, high rope act. This act is very thrilling, running some 15 minutes. The rope is 30 feet from the ground. Among the feats performed by this aerial artist are: walking blindfold standing on head, walking on stilts, riding a bicycle, walking blindfold with bag over his head and his feet in a bag, walking in cheese boxes and carrying a pail of water on his head. With a continuous performance of this kind going on throughout the day, public interest will never flag . . .

June 10 1901

In connection with the July celebration here a band tournament will be held on Farmers' Day. A prize of $100 is given to the winner. It is expected that Calgary, Canmore, Banff, Olds and Edmonton bands will compete. In addition the Edmonton band will furnish music every day.

June 10 1901

The directors would again ask citizens to have their residences decorated during the celebration. Large supplies of bunting have been brought in by merchants for this purpose.

Farmers having tents are also advised to bring them in as accommodation in town no doubt will be taxed beyond its limit.

June 14 1901

Around the Fair Grounds.

All the booths under the grandstand, 15 in all, have been let. The grandstand is now completed. It is one of the best structures of its kind west of Winnipeg. From it the entire stretch of track may be seen.

June 21 1901

A feature of Citizens' Day at the fair will be a football match between the fat and lean men. The fats are to be over 200 lbs. and the leans less than 125.

On Farmers' Day all children carrying flags will be admitted to the grounds free of charge. The Hudson's Bay Company offer to give flags to all children applying at their store on the morning of Farmers' Day.

During the four days of the fair, local merchants will close their stores at 12:30 noon. The public are requested to do their shopping early in the day. Parties having tents and coming to the fair would do well to bring them and so relieve the pressure on the hotels.

June 21 1901

The Fair

The visit of Col. Dent on July 2nd to purchase horses for the British army is an attraction that is not on the bills.

The Edmonton Industrial Exhibition Association, Ltd.

FIRST ANNUAL FAIR.

If You Miss it You'll Regret it.

ALBERTA'S

GRAND SUMMER FAIR

AT EDMONTON

JULY 1st to 4th, Next.

1st day, Citizens' Day.   -   3rd day, Farmers' Day.

2nd day, Old-Timers' Day. -   4th day, Americans' Day.

$5,000 IN PRIZES WILL BE OFFERED.

$5,000 Will be spent on New Buildings.

5,000 50-Page Prize Lists will be Distributed.

5000 People Will be There.

Are you Coming?
Do you intend to Exhibit?
Do you want a Prize List?
Do you want any Information?
Have you any Suggestions to Make?

If so, write to the Secretary,

A. G. HARRISON,

Edmonton, Al'berta.

July 6 1901

Edmonton's first summer fair has come and gone and despite a combination of unfortunate and adverse circumstances the fair was not a failure. The directors played in hard luck. In the preliminary arrangements they were delayed and interfered with by rain. Then, when the rain ceased, and everything was ready for the opening, the strike took place and all trains from Calgary were cancelled.

. . . . . the train was to bring north many fast horses to compete in the speeding events, . . . as well as the fire brigade band from Calgary and the Ponoka baseball team. All the fruit for the booths and track was lying at Calgary with no means of transport. In spite of all this the fair opened with a good attendance. Monday, 2,000 paid admission to the grounds.

Wednesday was to be Farmers' Day but the weather made other arrangements.

Americans' Day passed off quietly, the only disturbance being the occasional discharge of an old brass cannon borrowed from the Hudson's Bay Company, or the exploding of some sticks of dynamite. Five sticks were set off at seven o'clock Thursday morning on the market square creating a most terrific din.

July 8 1901

The Indians who have been making day and night melodious from their camp near the park gates, folded their tents and silently flitted late Sunday afternoon.

As the last fairgoers stole silently away the editor of the Bulletin was feeling a tender nostalgia for a simpler time which he and the Indians had lived together. It was 1901. Edmonton, home of The Big Fair, had a population of 2,628. Strathcona, home of Northern Alberta's Great Industrial Fair, had 1,550. Calgary, home of the Inter Western Pacific Exposition, had 4,091. It was understood by all true boosters of course that these figures were totally inadequate, vile slanders upon the civic greatness of the communities maligned, shrunken fantasies bred in the diseased minds of the official Dominion Census takers.

Edmonton's population was no 2,628. We had clearly twice that many, with more arriving daily.

Pleased by the splendid new grounds on the flats the editor noted with sadness how urban sprawl was overrunning Edmonton's historic sports field, around 102nd Avenue and 103rd Street:

> The old race track, one of Edmonton's historic spots, is rapidly passing away, having been divided by the owners, the Hudson Bay Co., into town lots and placed on the market.

> This was Edmonton's first circular track, previous to that all races having been run on the Victoria Trail or along the river brow in front of what is now the brick school house. Many interesting and exciting events have been pulled off on the old track. Of the early days, when Rowdy came up from the south and went back with all the honors and her owner's pockets bulging with the coin of the northern sports, the old timers tell in reminiscent mood.

> The old track was the birth place of Edmonton's athletic sports. Here Wm. West, Ed. Looby, Northwest and Skeezik competed in the foot races as far back as Dominion Day '82 . . . .

> In the bright summer evenings might be seen athletics competing in football, lacrosse, baseball and cricket while an occasional open-air concert by the band added to the attractions of the scene.

> Now all is changed; the old is giving way to the new. On the course where once the old grandstand stood, and on the green where for the last twenty years athletes have battled for supremacy in honest sport, in many games, villas are going up and boulevards will be laid out. Over the old course, where in the days gone by the wiry Indian cayuse champed his bit in eagerness to get away, shirt-waisted men will soon be wheeling modern babies in pneumatic-tired carriages down twentieth-century pavements.

The snows of another winter fell on old and new. Town Council voted to waive $70.95 due from the exhibition association, taxes on the new buildings at the fair grounds. And when the snows succumbed to spring breezes plans were afoot for a fair bigger than ever.

May 5 1902

A meeting of the directors of the Industrial Exhibition was held on Saturday evening, May 3, in the Board of Trade rooms. All correspondence read. The secretary was instructed to write Mr. Dorker, Calgary, re a cowboy show; R. Tacker, Lacombe, re pipers; town council re land for waterworks; and the CPR for passengers and freight rates for July 1, 2, 3.

July 4 1902

On the morning of July 1st the sun rose in all his (sic) glory and to the satisfaction and delight of everybody, for this was a double event — Dominion Day and the opening of the fair. At an early hour the farmer folks commenced to come in; these together with the numerous visitors . . . . gave the main street a busy appearance.

The hotels were crowded to their full capacity to accommodate the strangers who arrived on Monday, and who registered over 150 names. Soon gaily decorated buses appeared on the scene to carry the sightseers to the beautiful exhibition grounds on the river flat . . . .

The exhibitors and competitors both man and beast, had entered into the spirit of the enterprise, for it is an enterprise and one on which the prosperity of a western town largely depends . . . .

July 7 1902

F. F. Tims, secretary of the Edmonton Exhibition Association, received a wire on Wednesday from Calgary stating that owing to the bad weather and the roads in the south the fair to be held there was postponed until September 1st.

July 21 1902

The date of the Strathcona fair has been postponed from August 7th and 8th to August 8th and 9th. The 9th is Coronation Day and a public holiday and the loyal people of Strathcona desire that their fair should be part of a world wide celebration.

July 28 1902

Strathcona: The hay crop on the agricultural grounds was sold by tender to P. M. Barber for $81.

August 1 1902

The annual fair of the Fort Saskatchewan agricultural society will be held on Wednesday and Thursday the 13th and 14th inst. Prizes are offered for stock exhibits. There is an attractive list of horse races and a grand baseball tournament for a silver cup valued at $50, presented by J. W. Shera MLA. Competition open to all organized baseball clubs in Alberta.

August 25 1902

Advertisement: Edmonton Industrial Exhibition Association

Every shareholder who is in arrears is hereby warned that every share held by them will be cancelled if balance due is not paid by them in person on or before Friday night the 29 inst.

The directors are giving this final notice, although not bound to do so as every person has been notified before.

By order,

F. Fraser Tims, secretary.

September 19 1902

From the Calgary Herald, commenting on the Inter-Western Pacific Exhibition:

We are only expressing the opinion of everyone that the recent exhibition was in almost every way a failure. It was a waste of public money contributed to its programme; and . . . . it did harm to the city and the surrounding country. As to the vegetables, there were such a limited number of them that strangers went away with the impression that they were curiosities in this part of the world.

Coming to the attractions these were weak, and the horse races disappointing to say the least, and had it not been for the baseball games the public would probably have demanded their money back.

September 26 1902

A meeting of the Edmonton Exhibition Association was held in the secretary's office on Saturday evening. The solicitor was instructed to transfer to the town 2½ acres purchased for waterworks purposes, the price being $1,000.

On January 28 1903 the town took title to 1.94 acres of the southwest corner — Land Title certificate 31-Y-1. Part of the main power plant is there now. Town Council also waived taxes on the fair ground buildings, which had climbed in value to $222.

January 29 1903

New Agricultural Society: A meeting was held in Vegreville school house on Monday January 12 to take steps to organize an agricultural society in that locality. R. D. Dunwoodie was chairman and Dr. Goodwin secretary. Both are late of Edmonton. Fifty names were sent to the department of agriculture at Regina with the petition for organization. It is confidently expected that the society will have a successful career as it has a very large and progressive settlement from which to draw support.

Looking south towards Strathcona. Railbirds await the racing horses while a little girl minces daintily across an impromptu bridge.

March 9 1903

The following are the dates arranged at the conference on Thursday last for Alberta fairs from Edmonton to Calgary.

Edmonton, June 30 and July 1st and 2nd.

Wetaskiwin, July 3rd and 4th.

Calgary, July 7th to 10th.

Strathcona, Aug. 13th and 14th.

Fort Saskatchewan, Aug. 17th and 18th.

Lacombe, Aug. 20th.

Olds, Oct. 6th.

Innisfail, Oct. 7th.

Red Deer, Oct. 8th and 9th.

A late entry was to be at Vegreville on October 10th, first fair of the new Vermilion Valley and Battle Lake Agricultural Society.

ALBERTA'S GRAND SUMMER FAIR, EDMONTON,

**Livestock parade northwards, towards the heights of Edmonton with MacKay
Avenue School dominating the skyline.**

March 29 1903

From The Eye Opener: (Fabled humorist Bob Edwards was pub-
lishing his paper in High River): The secret of the never failing success of the Edmonton fair is that the management is not too stuck
up, religious or hypocritical to take official cognizance of the race
horse man. The horsemen are treated royally and squarely when they
get there and the purses are paid right away when won.

April 21 1903

The Edmonton Industrial Exhibition Association at its meeting
last night decided to close with the Hand Fireworks Company of
Hamilton, Ontario for a two nights display of fireworks including an
exposition of Baden Powell's armored train, the first display of its
kind given in Canada.

51

(This was the forerunner of the electronic scoreboard of today. Colored fireworks were mounted on a large metal net and programmed to represent a dramatic event, such as a highlight in the African campaigns of Britain's great soldier, Lord Baden-Powell, later founder of the Boy Scouts).

April 23 1903

From The Eye Opener: On June 30th, July 1st and 2nd Edmonton has her annual exhibition. It bids fair to be a corker with $10,000 hard cash in prizes, $4,000 of which goes to the horse races. The clerk of the course, Mr. Barney Cooper has sent cordial letters of invitation to all the horse men of the West to come and compete, laying stress to the necessity of square dealing on both sides. Nor is this clerk of the course above seeking suggestions from the horse men themselves as to suitable races and suitable distribution of the purse
. . . . .

As for the exhibition end of it, the $6,000 prize money will attract exhibitions from near and far, and the exhibits will be the best the country can produce.

Calgary fair comes a week later when everyone will be broke. We fear Edmonton is outfiguring Calgary as she did in the notorious hockey match a short time back.

May 2 1903

Nor'West Farmer: The Edmonton Industrial Exhibition is destined to become one of the great annual events of the future and will exert a powerful influence on the development of this portion of the West. The association has a capital stock of $20,000 fully subscribed and so prosperous has the show been that the shares have doubled in value in three years.

May 19 1903

The directors of the Edmonton Industrial Exhibition Association held their regular meeting in F. F. Tims' office last night. The contract for the construction of a dining hall 30 X 100 feet was awarded to Wm. J. Carter. A building 40 X 16 will be erected on the grounds in which to store the material for the great fireworks display. The secretary is still in correspondence with a view to securing further attractions. A world famous bicycle rider and his wife have been engaged to perform marvelous bicycle tricks.

June 9 1903

From the Eye Opener: Look in another column for our advertisement of the Edmonton Industrial Exhibition . . . No ghastly attempt will be made to make a feature of lemonade as they propose doing at the Calgary fair.

June 11 1903

A bus will leave the Alberta Hotel at 7 o'clock this evening for the exhibition grounds. All baseball players are requested to turn out to practice.

Council meeting: A question of a grant to the Edmonton Exhibition Association was discussed and it was unanimously agreed to vote $1,000.

June 30 1903

About seven hundred people arrived in Strathcona from the south last evening to attend the Edmonton Exhibition.

It looked bad for the fair last night when it began to rain but the looks were the worst part of it as only a light sprinkle fell.

During the fair there will be four trains a day between Edmonton and Strathcona. In addition to the regular time card trains, an extra will leave Edmonton at eleven o'clock every night.

(By this time Edmonton had train service — of sorts. The fabled Edmonton Yukon and Pacific Railway had been run from Strathcona down Mill Creek ravine, over the Low Level Bridge, to a depot at the foot of McDougall Hill).

July 2 1903

Edmonton celebrated the 36th birthday of this glorious Dominion of Canada yesterday by the second day of her great exhibition. All the principal stores and houses were gaily decorated with bunting and flags of all kinds. The weather was the unfortunate feature as it was showery throughout the day. This was all the more exasperating when it was known that St. Albert, a few miles to the north, and Strathcona to the south, were enjoying sunshine.

It took days to publish the names of the winners. There were literally hundreds in all categories, but it was important to the country that each be given recognition by the press. W. Wakeford of Clover Bar who won a silver teapot donated by Tetley Teas for the best ten pounds of butter in prints. John Gainer of Strathcona who won first prize for the best fat steer. Mrs. Ed Looby, the blacksmith's wife, who made the best lampshade. J. Kantz who grew the best round radish and Donald Ross who showed the best long radish. While Soldiers and politicians sought medals of bronze, gold and silver, exhibitors at the fair were satisfied with a prize of lead — fashioned into letters to proclaim them winners.

There go the pacers!

January 2 1904

Ottawa: Honourable Clifford Sifton has arranged with his colleagues to give a grant of fifty thousand dollars to the Dominion exhibition at Winnipeg, next summer. The ministry is arranging to get the Canadian Manufacturing Association and the Winnipeg Exhibition Association to cooperate.

March 26 1904

The Exhibition Association have already purchased and now have on the fair grounds seven tons of timothy hay for use during the fair. The hay was furnished by T. Daly of Clover Bar.

April 28 1904

A special supplement today features the Canadian Exhibit at the St. Louis World's Fair.

May 3 1904

Calgary now has two automobiles.

Here come the thoroughbreds!

May 11 1904
   Town council meeting: A communication from the Secretary of the Exhibition Association asking to have the water turned on at once in the grounds for the convenience of horsemen . . . was left to the town engineer.

June 1 1904
   Cheap rates will be put in force on all Canadian railways in connection with the Dominion of Canada exhibition and the same will be sufficiently extended to enable people to see the Canadian West.

June 21 1904
   Many alterations have been made in the grounds and buildings . . . in preparation for the big fair next week. A (wooden) sidewalk has been constructed by the town from the (railroad) depot to the main entrance, doing away with the unpleasant tramp through dust or mud which has been one of the drawbacks . . . .

June 29 1904

In anticipation of the coming fair and the opportunity afforded by it, all sorts and conditions of men, some of them not desirable parties to have in town, have been arriving daily. For several days the police have been marking those who were apparently here for no good errand and the chief has been distributing the red ticket which means "Twenty four hours to get out of town."

A consignment of six were sent down the line last week with an invoice to the Calgary police that they might assist them in keeping on the move.

July 1 1904

FIRST DAY OF THE FAIR
LARGEST FIRST DAY CROWD OF RECORD

It was estimated that at one time in the afternoon there were in the neighborhood of 5,200 people on the grounds, . . . about 500 in excess of the attendance on the opening day last year.

July 1 1904

FIREWORKS LAST NIGHT

(The display) began with a battery of resonating shells, followed by flights of rockets . . . These were followed by fountains from which were thrown streams of colored fire and mottoes appropriate to the occasion. The first of these was "Edmonton Welcomes You" spelled out in large letters with lights changing as they burned in various colors. The second was a very beautiful design, "Peace and Prosperity to the Tiller of the Soil" and brought cheers and applause from the spectators.

July 4 1904

EXHIBITION HALL
A PALACE OF BEAUTY
LARGE EXHBITIS IN ALL CLASSES.
ATTRACTIVE ARRANGEMENTS OF
ADVERTISING DISPLAYS

A very interesting display was that of the Edmonton Brewing and Malting Company. A complete line of their manufactures was shown. A very attractive part of this display was the word "Edmonton" lettered in barley and the word "Beer" in hops.

July 5 1904

The directors and members of the exhibition association are jubilant over the results of the fair. One of the complimentary features . . . was the splendid order which prevailed. Out of a total attendance of over 20,000 people, only three drunks came up yesterday for trial.

July 20 1904

In previous years the special constables on the exhibition grounds during the fair were paid three dollars a day. This year the men were paid off at two dollars a day. They took their grievances to the town (council) last night . . . .

July 28 1904
City Council:
A new problem confronted the city fathers, that of limiting the speed at which automobiles may travel on streets of the town. The solicitor was instructed to draw up a bylaw covering this.

There's a contradiction here. Edmonton is called city and town in the same story. True, it was still a town but the councillors were working to upgrade its civic dignity, at which they succeeded in December, so they are properly called "city fathers."

Then, early in 1905, rumors spread southwards that a civic institution was threatened:

March 10 1905 — the Albertan

The Edmonton fair has been a credit to the west and that it should be discontinued will be a serious misfortune, not only for Edmonton but for the entire west.

But it was only a rumor.

March 16 1905 — the Bulletin
Edmonton's Big Fair will be held on June 29, 30 and July 1st.

May 3 1905
The directors of the Exhibition Association have arranged for even better fireworks than usual . . .

June 16 1905
Arrangements for the Big Fair which opens on June 29th proceed rapidly. Entries are pouring in and the sale of booth space passes all records. Five horses have already arrived to go in training for the races and three more are expected in tonight.

June 23 1905
The Edmonton Exhibition Association will take all necessary steps to protect the ladies' exhibits from being handled by the public.

June 29 1905

THE GATES OPENED.
EDMONTON'S BIG FAIR IS ON.
MECHANICAL TURNSTILES FOR THE FIRST TIME.

July 21 1905 — The Albertan
   Calgary is not boasting of its righteousness but Calgary people and people of the west, in the light of the recent gambling carnival in Edmonton regard the people of Edmonton as the most depraved in the West, and the press of that town as the most cowardly for not exposing the outrage and insisting on its removal.

July 31 1905 — The Calgary Herald
   Tinhorn gamblers around Calgary might as well understand that the vagrancy law will be applied to them. They have their choice — Edmonton or Butte.

October 9 1905 — The Strathcona Plain Dealer
   Reverend A. M. MacDonald preached in the Baptist church on Sunday evening from 1st Timothy 1-8. He said that agricultural fairs when properly conducted were stimulating and elevating but denounced in strong incisive language the methods by which some of these fairs were now conducted. He mentioned the Edmonton fair and Strathcona races as examples and praised . . . the town police for the prompt manner in which they stamped out the objectionable features of the *Strathcona* races.

Now why should Edmonton's sophistication in the matter of gaming invite such scornful attack? Especially from the Albertan, which, only months before, was lamenting unfounded rumors of our fair's demise? No doubt this is the reason, a headline in the Bulletin:

July 25 1905
INAUGURATION OF PROVINCE TO BE HELD AT
EXHIBITION GROUND!

The most exalted dignitaries in Canada would soon be heading west, to inaugurate Alberta as a province and Edmonton as *capital city*. Towns less worthy of the honor were simply jealous over the headline in the Bulletin, of which Frank Oliver was editor. Since 1879 we have been watching the growth of Edmonton and its fair through news reports in the Bulletin. At the time for selection of the capital, Frank Oliver happened to be in Ottawa as member of parliament and member of the federal cabinet as well. Boosters of Calgary and other less-deserving towns seemed to think Frank Oliver being in the cabinet had given Edmonton some kind of advantage.

1905-09 *Growing Pains*

Properly excited at being capital of a new province the city of Edmonton went riding off in all directions, expanding east, north and west to accommodate the expected hordes of newcomers.

To keep an eye on historical developments in this frantic period more avenues of information open up. To now the only source has been the Bulletin, published by Frank Oliver whose presence in the federal cabinet had nothing to do with Edmonton's becoming capital. But from this point on there are stories in a rival paper called the Journal. Minutes of the Exhibition Association begin. The story is also found in minutes of the city council. The young city was getting into a number of services which older cities left to private chance: telephones, electric power, a street railway, a hospital. The summer fair was so important to Edmonton's image it was not surprising that the council should get involved in that too.

December 11 1906
Address of Donald Ross, president, to annual meeting of the Exhibition Association:

Gentlemen, as president of this association it devolves upon me to make a few remarks as to what has been done by your directors during the past year.

As a matter of fact they had rather a blindfold proposition, or rather propositions, to tackle. In the first place, acting in accordance with the resolution adopted at our last general meeting, they offered to the city for the sum of $30,000 the grounds of the association for park or recreation purposes. This the city council, with an ingenuity and fertility of imagination in discovering objections to even seriously entertaining the offer, or putting it before the ratepayers for their opinion upon the matter, completely turned down.

December 23 1905, The Bulletin
The news became general about the city this morning that the majority of the stock of the Edmonton Industrial Exhibition Association has changed hands. Messrs. McDougall and Secord are the purchasers and it is stated that they have acquired not less than 400 of the 600 shares . . . at about 40 dollars a share. When seen about the matter this morning Messrs. McDougall and Secord stated that it was their intention to offer the property to the city and that they hoped the exhibition would be carried on the same way as heretofore and under the same management.

January 2 1906, City Council:
Alderman Bellamy suggested the importance of taking steps for the purpose of holding an exhibition this year, and it would be necessary to endeavor to make arrangements either for acquiring the land upon which the exhibition was held . . . or a suitable site elsewhere.

January 9 1906, City Council:
Re proposed purchase of the Edmonton Industrial Exhibition Grounds:
Mr. J. H. Morris briefly addressed the council and made the following offer on behalf of the association: They were willing to lease the grounds etc. to the city for $3,000 for one year with an option to purchase at the end of that period for $60,000.
Moved Ald. Griesbach-Bellamy:
That the offer . . . be accepted . . .

January 22 1906, The Bulletin
The prospect is that the Fair for 1906 will be held under the auspices of the city. One point may be considered essential — the fair must be held. On this there is only one opinion in the council or out of it.
Edmonton's Big Fair has become the annual outing for the district and an event of consequence in the western year, which could be suspended only at a tremendous loss of prestige and sacrifice of material welfare.

January 29 1906, The Bulletin
The Winnipeg Telegram opines that Winston Churchill "is a lightweight of the most pronounced type and he never will be anything else."

February 19 1906, the Exhibition
It was decided to call the Fair of 1906 the "First Provincial Exhibition of Alberta" to be held on the 2nd, 3rd, 4th and 5th of July.

May 3 1906, the Exhibition
Secretary was instructed . . . to write Mr. Chapman of N. Battleford and offer him $100.00 for bringing his mare as an attraction.

As preparations advanced for the provincial fair events on the street reflected increased dignity of a capital city.

June 13 1906, The Edmonton Journal
Another broncho-busting exhibition on First Street this morning attracted the crowd. Although we are sorry to interfere with a good show we would like to inform the sportive horsemen, whose skill is the wonder of the everyday citizen, that First Street is a public thoroughfare.

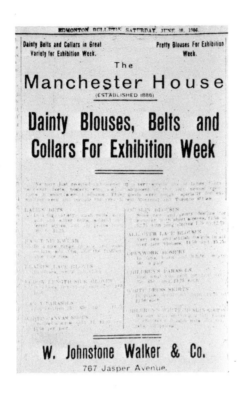

June 13 1906, the Exhibition

Mayor C. May notified the meeting that Mr. Barnes representing some association was in town and it would be a good chance to "get after him for a grant."

June 23 1906, The Bulletin

The women's aid of the city hospital are making preparations for serving meals on the grounds during the four days of the fair. Provisions are being donated by ladies of the city and country. Last year a number of friends from the surrounding country showed their interest in the work by supplying butter, eggs etc. and we hope they will not forget the hospital this year. Donations may be left at the home of Mrs. Fred Ross, corner of 14th and Victoria Streets.

July 2 1906, The Bulletin

GREATEST RACES EVER HELD IN ALBERTA
HORSES COMING FROM ALL OVER CANADA
ONE HUNDRED DOLLARS FOR THE FREE-FOR-ALL HORSE
WHICH BREAKS TRACK RECORD

Horse racing has been horse racing ever since the first Indian on the hurricane deck of a cayuse chased his red brother over the plains for the blankets and pemmican. History does not record that anyone ever came to Edmonton looking for a race and went away disappointed.

July 4 1906, The Bulletin

Edmonton's Big Fair has been running two days under the most favorable auspices and with every appearance of unqualified success.

Signs of the Times

DOGS Running At Large Will Be Shot On Sight

DRINK HARTLEY'S CIDER

Meanwhile, back at city hall — which was really the second floor of the fire hall on 98th Street:

Near the beginning of this chapter Alderman Bellamy had proposed to his fellow councillors that they buy either the existing fairground or a suitable site elsewhere. Apparently unable to choose they did not fall into the bog of indecision and buy neither. They bought both.

On January 7 1907, two days before the option expired on the Rossdale site, they bought it for $60,000 and the transfer was recorded by Land Title Certificate 45-Q-5. The other purchase was a little more complicated leaving no minutes to quote because it was done in secret. Bellamy and Co. wanted to buy a park site west of the city limit and a fairground to the east. Because it wasn't exactly legal to do so, and because they wanted to keep prices down, they met in the CNR dispatcher's office, appointed themselves *(as individuals)* agents for themselves *(as a city council)* and took options on the sites. On August 15 1906 the ratepayers voted in favor of Bylaw 63, in which Coronation Park was bought for $18,000 and the present exhibition site for $24,500. As owners of two fairgrounds the city fathers then set about ensuring the next show on site number one. They decided broader participation would guarantee success and involved the Board of Trade. But having three factions partly in control was a guarantee of something else:

June 7 1907, the Exhibition Association
   Re commissioners' letter on hospital dining hall. This letter was read and a motion made by Mr. J. H. Picard that in the opinion of the directors the Council have exceeded their authority in granting free rent to the Hospital Society.

Friction aside, headlines and stories in the Bulletin cause anticipation of success and confirmed it.

June 4 1907
   VEGREVILLE WILL COME TO THE FAIR.
   "SPLENDID BAND" FROM VEGREVILLE.

June 23 1907
   The Department of Agriculture will have a tent on the fairgrounds during the entire exhibition week. There will be an exhibit of the noxious weeds of the province. Lectures on poultry will be given from time to time by an expert from the Department.

July 1 1907
SECOND PROVINCIAL FAIR OFFICIALLY OPENED THIS AFTERNOON.
IMPRESSIVE CEREMONIES MARK THE FORMAL OPENING OF ALBERTA'S GREATEST.
THOUSAND GREET LIEUT.-GOV. BULYEA AND PARTY
AS THEY ENTER UNDER MILITARY ESCORT.
PERFECT WEATHER.

An auto race churns up dust.

July 2 1907
OPENING DAY CROWDS MORE THAN DOUBLE LAST YEAR.
FULLY 7,500 FILLED THE EXHIBITION GROUNDS ON MONDAY.
ALBERTA'S PROVINCIAL FAIR GRANDER THAN EVER.

July 4 1907
IMMORAL SHOW CLOSED.
    The objectionable feature of the midway . . . ceased doing business at 5 o'clock yesterday afternoon. After that hour "The Great Lepatha" was not permitted to further insult the unsuspecting public enticed into the tent to witness the performance by the innocent-sounding assurances of the manager that the show was a good one.

The woods east of the grounds offer cool shade for competing livestock and the horses of the crowd.

There was much to cheer about, but looking ahead to next year when Edmonton would have to compete with Calgary hosting the *Dominion* Fair, and to the years beyond that, it could be seen clearly that a more stable organization was required. Concern about the future led to this:

February 7 1908, the Exhibition
   Minutes of the meeting called for the purpose of the reorganization of the Edmonton Industrial Exhibition . . .
   Moved by Mr. Geo. Manuel & seconded by Mr. John A. McPherson that the capital stock of the association be $1,000, divided in 200 shares of $5 each fully paid, no one individual to hold more than one share. Carried.
   Moved by Mr. Geo. Manuel & seconded by Mr. D. R. Stewart that the number of directors be 20, ten to be elected by the Association & ten from the following bodies: City Council 2, government 2, board of trade 1, Stock Breeders Ass. 1, Poultry Breeders Ass. 1, Canadian Manufacturers Ass. 1, Horse Breeders Ass. 1, Sheep & Swine Breeders Ass. 1. Carried.

One of the prime attractions of western fairs came in for regrouping at the same time:

February 15 1908, the Calgary Herald
The formation of the Western Canada Turf Circuit which took place at Moose Jaw on Friday last is one of the greatest events that has taken place in the annals of racing in Western Canada. The idea originated with James E. Reilly of the Calgary turf club and that gentleman was loyally supported in the matter by the turf club, whose members were the prime movers in the concern.

March 31 1908, City Council
Moved Ald. Manson-Armstrong . . . that the (Exhibition) Association be informed that the city is anxious that they should perfect the organization and that they notify the city of their present status.

April 15 1908, the Exhibition
J. H. Morris the President of the Provincial Board of Directors, declared the meeting open at 4 p.m.
The Provincial President reported that the Provisional Board had taken the re-organization in hand and that the following had been accomplished:
Charter secured.
97 Members for the New Association . . .

And here is the document Joe Morris showed the assembled gathering. Just hours old, it was the birth certificate of the Association that still existed in 1979.

Certificate of Incorporation

I hereby certify that

The Edmonton Exhibition Association Limited

is this day incorporated under The Ordinance of the North-West Territories respecting Companies, and that the company is Limited.

Given under my hand and seal at Edmonton this Fifteenth day of April 1908.

Harold W. Riley
Registrar of Joint Stock Companies

Armed with this document the boosters went to work sending an exhibit to the Dominion Fair and putting on a good show of their own. On the day their fair opened in prospects of fine weather the Bulletin had news of a monster tomorrow:

BIG PARADE TOMORROW

The street parade that will be given at 10 a.m. by the Campbell Brothers Consolidated shows will be a brilliant spectacle consisting of hundreds of high-spirited horses with their natty trimmings. South American gauchos and Australian boomerang throwers; brighteyed senoritas from Mexico; desert-born bedouin Arabs; Japanese athletes and Hindoo fakirs; detachments of cavalry troopers of many flags; master horsemen of the universe; Mexican, Indian and American bands and strange Oriental music of many nations; funny clowns with their funny mules and ponies and the magnificent cages containing the wild beasts of the desert . . .

Perhaps this blurb contained just a tiny bit of exaggeration, a very slight overstatement of the marvels and wonders to be seen on Jasper Avenue but the cause was good and so were the results:

June 27 1908
SHOW RING TALK
All over for another year.
The best exhibition ever held in Edmonton.

This display had to impress visitors to the Dominion Fair in Calgary.

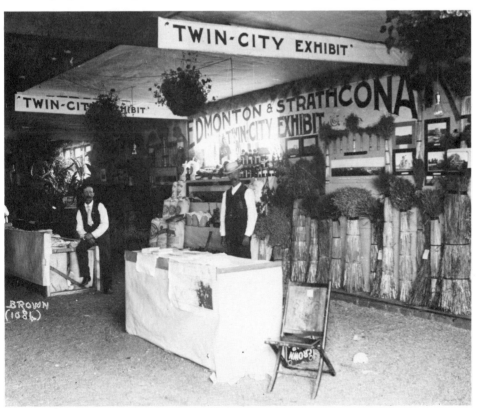

But looking to the future there was still a nagging weakness in the setup. Though the city took responsibility for grounds and buildings the show itself was still the personal burden of a few. The point was raised at the next annual meeting:

February 9 1909

The auditor's report was read dealing with the Association expenditure for the past 4 years amounting in all to some $20,000 . . . which the chairman (J. B. Mercer) pointed out was certainly not excessive in view of the immense amount of advertisement the city was getting. The chairman further pointed to the difficulty which the association had to contend with in the matter of financing, the directors having to endorse the paper of the association, and thereby reducing their credit in their own business.

The benefit of the exhibition was for the city as a whole and should be a direct tax on the residents. Mayor Robert Lee took up this same question and explained that the city was prepared to take a more lively interest in the exhibition work, and that facilities for financing more readily would be arranged for, subject to a larger percentage of the city representatives being on the board of directors.

Having accepted the principle they went about making it a mathematical formula. Forty percent of the directors should be appointed by the city, ten percent by the board of trade and fifty by the association. Percentages imposed a metric concept, multiples of ten. Twenty seemed about right, which meant the city named eight directors, the business community two, and of the association's allotment six were to be in charge of the agricultural aspect and four of the racing. That seemed to provide continuity on a year-to-year basis but there was still a weakness at day-by-day level. The only office staff was A. G. Harrison, secretary of the board of trade, who took minutes of exhibition meetings. So Mr. Harrison was hired as manager, the first full-time employee, and the boosters went about making the next better than ever.

June 28 1909, the Bulletin

FAIR OPENS TOMORROW
FOUR TIMES AS MANY ENTRIES AS ANY PREVIOUS YEAR

June 29 1909

INDIANS IN CAMP ON GROAT'S FLATS (west end of the Victoria golf course)
Three Hundred Came to White Man's Pow Wow
Will Be In Big Parade Today
Spent Free Time Riding Streetcars

July 3 1909

BIG CROWD WATCHED CLOSING DAY EVENTS
ATTENDANCE: 5,500 10,200 12,000 11,200 FOR FOUR DAYS

July 14 1909, from report of Manager A. G. Harrison

In my opinion the Exhibition should be treated as a business institution and should be held on grounds that can be made revenue producers not only for four days out of the year with a chance of dropping $10,000.00 through rain, but for 4 months of the year. To do this they should be located where they will be easy of access for baseball, football, general sports, outside shows, local race meetings, hospital bazaars, military drills, etc., and a percentage charged for their use. We should not then be entirely dependent on our 4 days exhibition for revenue but could make money throughout the year for the Exhibition Association and the City.

While the cause of agricultural fairs goes upwardly mobile, the cause suffers the loss of an important booster. Black edging is for Thomas Daley, pioneer farmer of Clover Bar and alderman of the city of Edmonton. In 1901 Mr. Daley became world oats king at the Paris International Exposition with oats sown at Clover Bar. In 1905 he grew apples on his farm. They may have been the first in Alberta. Thomas Daley thought they were. He put them up in jars and took them to fairs in Winnipeg, Chicago and Toronto to show doubters there really was a Garden of Eden on the frontier.

10 What a Glorious Site

Only thirteen months later new record crowds thronged the permanent site of the exhibition — if permanence can be construed as occupying the same location in the year of the centennial. The site had been bought and paid for through city council's clandestine plotting of 1906, but it was not, in fact, the favorite choice of the fair people. The burgeoning city had developed distinct east and west ends, with 101st Street as dividing line, and they hoped for a location more central — and less damp. Mr. Harrison liked the appearance of a 100-acre site up along 101st Street near 125th Avenue, but the owners demanded $300,000 in cash. However, everyone liked the general area so the city council appealed to the corporate citizenship of the Hudson's Bay Company. How would the gentlemen adventurers like to sell 100 acres of their Reserve at a reasonable price? In the *northeast* corner on the site of today's airport. The company countered with 95 acres in the *northwest* corner, along 121st Street, at $1,000 each.

The city fathers were not amused, and their annoyance was aggravated by the company's refusal to share the cost of draining Drunken Lake. This body of water was a slough which had got its name from the rowdier elements among early customers of Fort Edmonton. Upon trading their pelts and pemmican the swingers would retire to the lake and their celebrations gave it a name too picturesque for the Edmonton District Names Committee to perpetuate.

Rejected by the company the city fathers prepared to drain Drunken Lake by themselves and also to do something about Kirkness Lake, which made soggy the exhibition ground they had purchased in secret. Their determination was backed by an historic resolution:

> *September 14 1909, the City Council*
> *Moved Ald. Manson-Lundy:*
> That the new exhibition grounds, buildings and racetrack be constructed and erected on the east end park and that steps be taken at once to clean off the ground and have it properly surveyed and that sites for buildings and racetrack be located and that a bylaw to defray the expenses to the amount of $75,000 be prepared and submitted for the purpose of doing this work. CARRIED.

Following immediately on the heels of this resolution the city fathers established a committee with power to act on the good intentions. The action group included council's own parks committee, the city engineer and manager Harrison.

They decided to allow the maximum time for action and for one occasion only decided to hold the fair the last week in August. And to realize fully the possibilities of the triangular site they sought to tap the thinking of Edmonton's architectural community. Edmonton boasted eighty-five practicing architects, one for each 470 citizens, probably unmatched by any city in the civilized world. A design competition was announced, ideas to be submitted by February 10, and, as the notice stated, contestants were invited to set the bounds of their imagination as wide as they wished.

"The competitors are purposely given a wide scope to submit plans which will in their opinion be best suited to the grounds and to the present and future needs, on exhibition lines, of the growing city of Edmonton."

Ironically, it was not one of the city's practicing architects who copped the $250 first prize and saw his design etched upon the soggy terrain. Finding his profession overcrowded, Peter Rule had turned to contracting instead. Although the terms of the contest imposed no limits on the designer, the site did. An oval hump, almost an island, was the only possible place for the racetrack, so Peter placed it there, exactly where bettors find it now.

The boosters were busy building their grandstand and barns in the early months of 1910 but they were also building their organization, and in a masterpiece of the kind gave it incredible tensile strength — not two-ply strength, nor three-ply nor even four-ply but five-ply strength. And in the process they pulled a swifty on Calgary. On a single day in May they incorporated four breeder associations — for horses, cattle, sheep and swine — with head offices in the office of the exhibition association, and manager A. G. Harrison as secretary of all. So there was not one organization but five — interlocking, interacting — all for one and one for all — pulling together in the common cause. Now in regard to Calgary: the most prestigious name for any organization was Alberta or Provincial. Not content with either name the boosters appropriated both, so that Edmonton, seat of the provincial capital and University of Alberta, was also home of the Alberta Provincial Horsebreeders Association, and those for cattle, sheep and swine. Let Calgary editors copy that — and weep.

Through the months of May and June the contractors kept pace with the organization builders, and two months away from the opening of the fair the newspapers went to press with encouraging words:

June 30 1910

Work on the new exhibition grounds has been progressing rapidly during the last week. The race track has splendidly stood the heavy rains to which it has been subjected and half an hour after the heavy shower which occurred a few days ago was ready for use.
The water pipe has been conveyed to the grounds and will be laid in place this week.
The Exhibition Association have started their advertising campaign in earnest and advertisements are being inserted in all the papers in Alberta.

July 13 1910

RUSHING THE WORK AT THE EXHIBITION GROUNDS
DINING HALL WITH SEATING CAPACITY OF 500 PEOPLE
WILL BE STARTED THIS WEEK — THE GRANDSTAND WILL
BE COMPLETED IN A FEW DAYS
At Manager Harrison's request the C.P.R. will run a special stock train to Edmonton, picking up livestock at all points along the line. The Clover Bar, Humberstone, and Standard Coal Companies will give a large display of coal.

July 20 1910

MANY EXHIBITS AT FAIR — INDUSTRIAL AND COMMER-
CIAL DISPLAYS
There will be a three hundred dollar exhibit (of grasses) displayed by the exhibition association in conjunction with the board of trade. The provincial weed inspector, C. E. Lewis, will make an exhibit of noxious weeds.

73

August 1 1910

BIG EXHIBIT FOR THE EDMONTON FAIR
CARLOAD OF HORSES AND CATTLE FROM THE BIGGEST
STOCK FARM IN CANADA, AT LASHBURN, SASKATCHE-
WAN, WILL BE HERE.

August 17 1910

FAIR GROUNDS A BLAZE OF LIGHT
EXHIBITION BUILDINGS WILL BE BRILLIANTLY ILLUMI-
NATED AT NIGHT BY THOUSANDS OF INCANDESCENT
BULBS — A MINIATURE LAKE WITH ELECTRIC EFFECT AT
NIGHT WILL BE ONE OF THE ATTRACTIONS

The finishing touches are now being put on the new exhibition
grounds and all will be in readiness for the opening of the biggest fair
in Edmonton's history on Tuesday afternoon next. The grandstand,
upon which a double shift of men has been working for the past
week, will be completed without difficulty Monday night. Gravel
walks, green lawns, groves of trees and pretty flower beds will greet
the eye of the visitor . . . .

August 20 1910

EXHIBITION WILL BE A GREAT STOCK SHOW

That the Edmonton Exhibition next week will be essentially a stock
exhibition and will be the largest stock exhibition ever held in Northern Alberta, is indicated by the astounding figures displayed by the
official announcement of the entries in all classes. The stock entries
alone total 1,446 or 455 more than last year . . . . The eight cattle stables, the nine horse stables and the sheep and swine stables, all new
and modern, will be crowded to their capacity to accommodate the
stock that will be brought to the city next week.

August 20 1910

THE PROGRAM FOR THE WEEK

On the afternoon of the opening day a display of daylight fireworks
will form an attractive feature of the program. These consist of
bombshells which burst at a considerable height and discharge
various effects made of Japanese paper, such as floating fishes, floating animals, floating birds, floating men and women, showers of flags
and ribbons and mammoth confetti.

August 24 1910

Advertisement of the Burnham-Frith Electric Co.
AT THE EXHIBITION

IRONING BY ELECTRICITY cuts the labor in half and does away
with the hot kitchen which formerly made summer ironing torturous
and dangerous.
COME SEE THE IRON
and how simply it is operated.

Racing fans in the grandstand can look northeast to the paddock and the marquee where Walter Wilkins has near-beer for sale.

August 24 1910

EXHIBITION MARRED BY RAIN
SPECIAL TRAIN OF AL G. BARNES CIRCUS COMPANY
BOGGED IN MUD
TITANIC STRUGGLE BETWEEN MAN AND MUD WITH
TEAMS OF STRAINING, SWEATING HORSES AS THE INTER-
MEDIARIES

August 25 1910

TWENTY THOUSAND PEOPLE AT SECOND DAY OF
EXHIBITION
THE RECORD ATTENDANCE OF ANY PREVIOUS YEAR IS
DOUBLED
EDMONTON EXHIBITION NOW SECOND TO WINNIPEG
GREAT DIFFICULTY IS EXPERIENCED IN HANDLING
ENORMOUS CROWDS

The transportation of the enormous crowds was a big undertaking.
Both the C.N.R. and G.T.P. operated a half-hour train service
throughout the day. The C.N.R. sold over 5,000 tickets and the
G.T.P. over 5,000 (at 15 cents round trip from 101st Street and 104
Avenue). The street railway carried over 25,000 passengers (at 25
cents single fare). Fifteen cars were in commission, the last car leaving the grounds at eighteen minutes after midnight.

The service provided by the street railway was woefully inadequate . . . .

The people in the east end of the city suffered most. By the time the
cars from Strathcona and 21st Street reached First Street (they) were
crowded to such a degree that it was impossible for another
passenger to board them. Many people in the east end . . . in
ingenious desperation boarded the cars going in the opposite direction, proceeded to the terminus, and, remaining in the car were then
able eventually to reach the grounds. The worst congestion occurred . . . after the fireworks and other attractions were over.

A condition verging on panic occurred as each car came up to the sid-
ings and thousands surged to crawl in the doors of cars that wouldn't
hold hundreds . . . The worst crush happened a few minutes after
ten . . . One woman fell almost under the wheels of the moving car,
while her screams increased the excitement . . .

he roof of the grandstand commands a view of the livestock barns along the east fence and off over
e trees the exciting outline of a packing plant in North Edmonton.

11 Completing The Grand Design

In a few feverish months the exhibition moved not only from one site to another, but one era to another. In hectic 1910 Edmonton was at midpoint of its greatest effervescence, booming from six thousand boosters in 1906 to some 50 thousand in 1914. Edmonton was growing as never before, and never since. Even in the high-rise here-and-now Edmonton has not multiplied itself eight times in eight years. The boom pushed the exhibition to the remotest end, and pushed its history to a different method of telling.

To 1910 the history has been contained neatly in four-line reports of single events and one-line comments by crusty editors. But from here on it becomes a continuous, overlapping, interlocking web. Though there are still crisp headlines and crunchy quotes a narrative is required to hold events together, to tell, for a start, how the association went about completing the grounds to the grand design for which they'd paid Peter Rule $250.

The site was a triangle of sorts, with the apex pointing north on to 118th Avenue. The year 1910 had seen the rising of the grandstand along the south base, and along the northeast side the livestock barns, which, in the first world war would shelter Canadian soldiers and in the second would make billets for Air Force men of the British Commonwealth. At either end of the row of barns was to be a handsome building, at the apex of that triangle a Livestock Pavilion, and in the southeast corner a Manufacturers Building, where local processors of raw materials could literally and figuratively show their stuff. There was rich symbolism in this placement. Boosters looked to manufacturing to balance the economy of the new province, an economy overdependent on agriculture. The boosters had a motto: "The country needs payrolls." Before the war stalled the building boom, and young men like Peter Rule went off to fight, his grand design was achieved. And the boosters seeking to implant permanence never dreamed how permanent their work was to prove. The grandstand and Manufacturers Building were landmarks which endured for nearly half a century and the Livestock Pavilion, under another name, was still standing in 1979.

The city administration was deeply committed to the grand design and provided a money bylaw for $175,000. Mayor Charles May was named chairman of a building committee, along with Association directors Mr. East and Mr. West — James East and Bill West.

One of their first priorities in putting the site on a firm basis was making the ground itself more solid. The site was low and swampy. In the winter of 1911 five thousand yards of river gravel were moved in at $1.50 per cubic yard. Space for a show ring was made by filling a slough, but there was a constant nagging threat from Kirkness Lake. This body of water, east end counterpart of the south side's fabled McKernan Lake, occupied much of today's Borden Park. In winter, when Chinese lanterns hung in the trees and a band played for skaters, Kirkness Lake

One of the grand features of the Grand Design is the Manufacturers Building.

was a dream. But in summer it delighted neither eye nor nose, and when heavy rain raised the level it would ooze over into the fair grounds. The committee discussed the problem with Count Von Auberg, the courtly Austrian gentlemen who served the city of Edmonton as parks superintendent, asking him if he couldn't lower the level of Kirkness Lake. But the count still hadn't solved it when war broke out, and fearing internment as an enemy alien, took off for the far north and had to be rescued.

The Manufacturers Building reared its wooden octagonal head in time for exhibition of 1912. A lot of wood went into it — $5,370.31 worth supplied by Clark Lumber. It had so much class that in the fall the association decided to add a floor — a concrete pad worth $6,615.50.

The Livestock Pavilion took the most — time, money, sweat and tears, because it was to be solid brick — boosters loved to specify *solid* brick in calling for tenders, there was something so permanent about it. First discussed at a meeting on September 10 1910 it was barely ready for the fair of 1913. In three years the Pavilion was debated at more than thirty meetings, in which the directors voted on a confusing series of concepts and contracts.

The ideal structure of its kind was said to be at the Minnesota State Fair, in Hamline, Minnesota and manager Harrison was sent for a personal look at this Taj Mahal. Edmonton architects were invited to vie for the prestigious assignment of designing a local equivalent and top prize of $350 went to Rollie Lines. The building job was awarded on information supplied by Rollie but just what this was is shrouded in mystery. Even after the Pavilion was up the manager was vainly writing him for blueprints.

Inside the Manufacturers Building the Tetley's Tea booth gives a view of the grand staircase to the second level.

The building contractor was not one firm but a series of dissolving partnerships, which did not promote speed. In April 1912 the contractor of the moment brought all to a halt with dire predictions. The handsome brick walls would tumble like those of Jericho if the footings specified by the architect were not made heavier. So the directors said to broaden the footings to three feet square and deepen them to fifteen inches. A delay was threatened by the lumber supplier, who sent cedar ship-lap rather than spruce, but it was found that cedar would do if nailed in a novel manner. In the fall of 1912, a full two years after the decision to go, there was a plaintive resolution asking that work be pushed. However, the roof was the subject of a separate contract which required much learned discussion on the subject of roofs and their painting. Then there was lighting, with a vote in favor of incandescent followed by a contradictory vote in favor of arc lighting, with a contract awarded first to a Canadian supplier then to a British firm. All this time Edmonton was growing bigger and more city-minded and more fashion-conscious, and seating became a contention.

The spring horse show, above and beyond its equine purpose, was the social event of the season, an occasion for display of fashion finery. While the animals paraded on the sawdust there must be a proper promenade for the people of fashion who occupied the box seats. These were the city-bred newcomers who were taking control of Edmonton's affairs, squeezing out the tobacco-spitting oldtimers. The promenade had to be a broad walkway separating the boxes from the cheap seats. The grand design was agreed on but then came complaints that the woodwork on the boxes was too plain and coarse for leaders of society and it was

Inside the Livestock Pavilion the pick of the Percherons come to judgment.

redone. The boxholders had chairs. Three thousand cheap seats were bought at 93 cents each, benches with wooden slats and cast-iron frames. After all the travail the Pavilion was ready for the fair in August 1913, just in time for a shootout between horsemen and cattlemen for best times and days.

But as the project reached the final throes of completion a dramatic event downtown thrust an unpredictable destiny on the Livestock Pavilion. The event was a fire, a dead-of-night blaze that destroyed the Thistle Rink. The historic Thistle, on 102nd Street behind the King Edward Hotel, scene of all big events for a dozen years. Scene of grand speeches and concerts on the inauguration of the province. Scene of the first session of the first legislature. Of fancy-dress skating parties at which the Lieutenant Governor presided as patron after leading an unsteady grand march around the ice. Of hockey games at which fans threw coal on the ice to confound the enemy. The Thistle, with its rich lode of memories, went up in smoke and the boom of artillery blanks stored by the militia.

Edmonton needed a hockey rink and gathering place for all indoor events of large scale. And so the Livestock Pavilion became The Arena, and then The Edmonton Gardens, and remained Number One in its class until the Coliseum came along sixty-one years later. A. G. Harrison had urged the city to develop exhibition facilities which could be used four months of the year instead of four days. With the spectacular demise of the Thistle Rink the new grounds came into use through all four seasons.

12 The Greatest of These is Hockey ....

From the Edmonton Journal, December 23 1913

Joyfully associated with Christmas day are hockey, Santa Claus, turkey and numerous other things, but the greatest of these is hockey. Victoria Day has its ball games and horse races, Thanksgiving its rugby game, Dominion Day and Labor Day their athletic events, and last but not least the Yuletide treat to which the sportsman looks forward each year is the opening of the hockey season. Added importance is lent to the opening of the hockey season this winter by reason of the fact that Edmonton fans will be introduced to the new Arena at the exhibition grounds, the best in western Canada.

With destiny pointing the finger of greatness at their Livestock Pavilion, directors of the association decided to make hockey and skating a concession. They would ask for tenders, winner-take-all until March 15th when the ice would have to be thawed in preparation for the spring stock shows. There were two bidders, just the two you'd expect. Deacon White offered a thousand dollars and Shorty Campbell bid nine hundred.

Deacon was Edmonton's first sports executive, founder of the Eskimo football and baseball teams, and teacher of athletics. His business was a glittering pool hall on Jasper Avenue, a dignified emporium with a discreet backroom for sportsmen who fancied cards. Born and raised in Chicago, Deacon had never played hockey. Shorty on the other hand was one of the most active hockey players ever to do battle in the Thistle or Jimmy Smith's South Side Covered Rink. In an era of small rinks and seven-man teams a small man had to compete for his share of the ice, and Walter Campbell used his stick fiercely and freely to promote generosity in the matter of playing room. In the business line Deacon had only his pool hall but Shorty was active in building, lumber, coal, real estate and sporting propositions like race programs. When outbid for the hockey concession he showed he could stickhandle pretty well in the back room too, a skill he never lost.

To his friend the Deacon he made an offer so ingenious it couldn't be refused. Deacon should withdraw his offer, then Walter would get in for nine hundred dollars and they'd be partners. While Deacon managed the nobler aspects of sport Walter hung billboards from the rafters and sold all the advertising space before the first game. There was no heat in the building so the lessees were given permission to build waiting rooms with stoves, and to use any loose lumber they might find lying about the grounds. The box office was at the north end, close to the streetcars which ran along 118th Avenue. Box seats would cost a dollar, cheap seats would be 75 cents or 50 depending on location and kids would be free. but to keep the kids from upstaging the paying customers they would be held in a retaining room until just before the faceoff.

On Christmas Day 1913, some two thousand fans, equivalent of twenty thousand today, rode streetcars to the east end for their best-ever Yuletide treat. They were to see hockey on the biggest ice surface in Canada — 220 feet long, seventy feet more than the Thistle. Their view was unobstructed by the wire-mesh screen of the Thistle which had protected the players from the fans. Fans in box seats looked down on the action from a lordly elevation of six feet.

Pages 82-83 show the exterior of the Livestock Pavilion. Here is the earliest known inside view of the building as a hockey arena. Billboards advertising Sullivan's Dancing Academy and Lewis Brothers Cafe indicate the early 1920s. The goal judge, with the hat, stands on the ice behind the net, waiting to signal a goal by raising his right arm.

Around two p.m. referee Harold Deeton dropped the puck for the first faceoff on the big ice, the ice that would be an operating theatre for men of heroic stature like Shore, Keats, Gagne, Colville, Reardon, Clovechok, Hall, Ullman, Bucyck and others whose name is legion and legend. One of the greats was on the ice for the opening faceoff. Barney Stanley was a defenseman for the Dominion Furriers, and in goal behind him was Court May, brother of famous-flyer-to-be Wop May. The Dominions were opposed by the Eskimos, owned by Deacon and Shorty. The Eskimos took a 1-0 lead into the dressing room but the Dominions came out rushing in the second half — that's correct, the second half — and won 4-2. And the fans went home to their turkey dinners taking with them the very first memories of a hockey game at the Arena.

13 The Events

The ice-free months of 1911 offered the first chance to plan a full measure of activities on the big grounds. In April occurred the first public demonstration of that twentieth-century marvel, the aeroplane. In August the exhibition parade was a half-mile salute to the workhorses who pulled the wagons of Edmonton commerce.

Most events testified to society's continued dependence on the horses — for the heavy hauling, for light transport, and for thrilling spectator sport. There were eight days of racing in 1911, three at the spring meet in May, and more during the fair which was extended from four days to five. A standard card meant five races with intervals of not more than fifty minutes. A trotting event would open the afternoon, then a pace or trot followed by three running races. For patrons wishing to invest in their judgment of horses professional bookmakers operated on the track. Free enterprisers the like of R. C. Mitten, J. Carson and C. L. Jones bid against each other for a concession. The right to print race programs was also a concession, and Walter Wilkins won the franchise to sell two-percent beer by outbidding Frank Goode — at times when Goode didn't outbid Wilkins.

The aerial display was supposed to add entertainment to the spring livestock show and money to the exhibition's account at the Imperial Bank. Aviators Hugh Robinson and Bob St. Henri were hired to bring their Curtiss biplane on the train, put it together on the grounds and make three flights a day, circling the race track at a dizzying two hundred feet. "Hangers" were distributed far and wide announcing the dates: April 27 and 28. Large crowds were expected, and the crowds came all right, — but only as far as the fence. Cheapskates, of whom the city seemed to have a depressing number, could climb boxcars or trees and watch those magnificent men in their flying machine without paying.

People could be so damned annoying at times. Not so, horses. Horses were loyal and trustworthy and ever reliable. No wonder the workhorses of Edmonton were honored in the exhibition parade that year. August 16th was Citizens' Day. It was decided that the workhorses should enjoy a holiday like all other good citizens. They would be the parade.

The race meet gave horses named Cyclone a place in the sun. Stock shows gave horses named Aberystwyth Son of Kildonan the Second, a chance to shine. But these were aristocrats with papers. On Citizens Day 1911 common old working chaps named Dan and Freddie needed no papers to parade. The only entrance requirement was a wagon. Even a horse named Dan can shine like a walnut table, given an affectionate scrub and the full August sun. On August 16th three hundred of them formed up in the area where most found employment — in "the warehouse district" — along 102nd Avenue.

Some of the few who paid to see the Curtiss biplane.

The brass band of the 101st Fusiliers led the parade on to Jasper Avenue and up 96th Street and along 111th Avenue to the grounds. Horses with official commissions came first in parade order, the fire department teams and the "big ones" of the city works department. The old-timers came next, led by Pete and Jock, a pair of agile twenty-year olds. And in behind came a half-mile of horses, pulling brewery wagons, bakery wagons, coal wagons, transfer wagons, grocery wagons, milk wagons, construction wagons, brick wagons, department store wagons. All wagons were decorated, most newly painted. A coal dealer, a very minor dealer who effected deliveries with a single horse, rode an ancient high conveyance of a type popular in Ireland half a century before. On his horse he had hung a sign in the shape of a heart. It read: I'm No Kid but I'm Still In Harness. On they came, on to the grounds and once around the track past the grandstand where Humane Society judges had a gold medal to award the teamster with the best-cared-for horses.

Along the route drivers of upstart motor cars might honk horns in derision but the automobile, like the aeroplane, was still a plaything, too light for hauling and subject to breakdown without notice. Should a horse get stuck in the mud no one hired two automobiles to pull it out. On city street and country farm the horse turned the wheels of the economy.

Though the directors were eager to see greater use of the grounds they were most particular about the high-class nature of attractions to be allowed on. In 1912, when Guy Weadick was staging the first Calgary Stampede, a promoter named Maddison wanted to lease the grounds for a "wild west show" but was firmly rejected. Edmonton was trying to get rid of the "fur trade" image and was looking forward to the early demolition of Fort Edmonton. Barney Oldfield, most famous of all auto racers was also turned down when he tried to lease the racetrack for a riproaring show by his travelling circus of speed demons. The Edmonton Motorcycle Club was turned down. Promoter R. B. Russell wanted to stage a flying show but after their experience with the Curtiss Aeroplane the directors said no to that. Even Dame Nellie Melba, the renowned Australian singer, was not deemed of sufficiently high calibre to be assisted by the Ex. The promoter wanted to borrow chairs for Melba's concert downtown at the Thistle Rink but got the same reception as Barney Oldfield. The directors wanted the aura of class about proceedings at the new grounds. To that end they purchased fifteen white coats for the attendants, which occasioned some snide snickering. However, the white coats were not for the purpose snickered about. They were to be worn by grooms while parading animals at livestock shows. The animals never lacked class, but the people sometimes did. For example: The secretary was instructed to notify Mr. Spinks that the hackney horse Devondale in charge of a man named "Curley" must be shown by another man as "Curley" was prohibited from showing for two years.

The entire year 1912 was pervaded by an atmosphere of carnival. The all-night lineup to buy lots in the long-awaited sale of the Hudson's Bay Reserve. The jubilations marking the amalgamation of Edmonton with Strathcona, and merger of their competing institutions including the summer fairs. These were euphoric happenings found in no other year. A. G. Harrison left the manager's desk at the exhibition to become commissioner of the booming city of Edmonton and in to succeed him came a Toronto man, W. J. Stark, who was to be on the scene for years. On the outside of the new fence of the Exhibition grounds, a block-long sign was painted, where it would be seen by passengers arriving on trains of the Grand Trunk Pacific and Canadian Northern Railways. Train riders were advised that the dates of the 1912 fair were August 12 to 17.

With 1912 the exhibition became a six-day affair which it remained until 1967. Though the official opener came on Tuesday, and attendance was counted for five days — admission 75 cents till six p.m., 50 cents afterwards — Monday, known as Preparation Day, drew large crowds and in some respects was the most exciting day of all.

A Journal reporter, wandering among the crowds at "the model fair grounds of the Dominion," watching the attractions being brought in and set up, was moved to write that five thousand exhibits were in position "from manufactories to hens." And then he couldn't resist observing that hens "played no mean part in the manufacturing line themselves." The Journal had bought a motorcycle to race to the grounds with latest editions off the press and race downtown again with latest news from its reporters. The machine made a cylinder-popping run with that exhilarating prose.

The motorcycle roared again Tuesday afternoon to carry the official opening remarks of Honourable Duncan Marshall. The minister of agriculture welcomed all Canadians to the greatest exhibition Edmonton had ever seen and the greatest

Excitement is spelled horses! Mrs. O'Brien holds the reins on Senator at the spring show of 1913. On the race trace the famed western trotter Bland S. enters the home stretch in a challenge match with a thoroughbred.

cattle show ever seen in Alberta. Oh, some might contend that there were more cattle at the Dominion Fair in Calgary in 1908 but that was because special inducements had been offered to eastern exhibitors so it didn't count. He asked the cheering multitude to recall that only four short years ago the finest exhibition grounds in the west was wild land. Many thought Edmonton was too optimistic in the matter of cost ($27,100) and space (147 acres) and buildings but the growth of the city had warranted it. Thousands of homes could be seen from the grandstand which were not there a year ago, as anyone listening would agree (and they all did) and next year there'd be more, and the year after that.

Now that was the grand stuff — as Jim Ryan, the Irish real estate man would say — and every town and hamlet in Alberta felt the same rosy assurance of destiny's favour.

On Citizens' Day there was no parade. No one could come up with a theme to top the cavalcade of workhorses. Though there'd been some talk of a parade of decorated automobiles the city's eight hundred drivers were bitterly critical of the condition of the roads. However, the Journal motorcycle continued its high-speed chase:

> Everyone who has visited the fairgrounds this week proclaims it to be the best he's seen. The vast improvements in the grounds, the buildings for the exhibits and the beautifully kept walks call for praise that seldom falls on so young a city.
>
> The large cities of the east will have to look to their laurels if they wish to keep their names in front of the list of the Dominion's first class shows.
>
> Edmonton, progressive as she is in all her municipal policies, is as progressive in her annual exhibition. Forging ahead like an ocean leviathan the fair is plowing into the waves of criticism and emerging from the onslaught with her bows all untarnished and the good ship ready to embark on another voyage of enterprise.

These were facts, of course, but there was even more grand stuff when the figures were totalled. Attendance for the five paid days was 63,929 — up from 40,003 the summer before.

As plans were made for an even bigger blowout in 1913 the association rejected ideas put forth by the United Farmers of Alberta, and the dominant figure in prairie racing, E. L. Richardson of Winnipeg, but welcomed intervention by the government of the state of New York. Having won the fight with the frontier, Alberta's country people were organizing to gain political power. The UFA demanded that only bona fide farmers be allowed to vote at meetings of the exhibition association. But the notion violated the letter of the Joint Stock Companies Act, and the spirit of the exhibition itself. A few years later the spirit would be crystallized in the slogan: Where City and Country Meet. While the UFA sought to bar city folk from fair boards Mr. Richardson tried to bar "colored" jockeys and trainers from western racing. It was reaction to a knife incident at Moose Jaw involving a black trainer. There was a good deal of prejudice in the optimistic prairie air. Only three years earlier the Edmonton board of trade had tried to stop black immigration into Alberta. However, the exhibition board took the view that individuals might be barred from the track for cause, but there could be no blanket exclusion of any group. Not all curly-haired grooms had been banned from the showring because "a man named Curley" failed to come up to the high standard of his horse Devondale.

But about the state of New York. A series of gambling scandals caused the state to declare gambling illegal. The long-term effect, of course, was to make illegal gambling profitable, but in the short term it dumped a lot of gaming equipment on the market at bargain prices. The association had been thinking about pari-mutuel machines. Manager Stark was sent to New York. He bought ten machines for $900 and on the way home rented them to the Regina fair board for a week for $200. Instead of leasing the gaming concession to private operators the house would take a percentage of each pot.

On August 12 1913 newspaper headlines blazed:
GREATEST ASSEMBLY OF BLUE BLOOD STOCK EVER SHOWN IN PRAIRIES FILLS STALLS AND JUDGING RING. OFFICIAL OPENING BY DOMINION LIVESTOCK COMMISSIONER JOHN BRIGHT AT 2 O'CLOCK

But the pari-mutuel operators were too busy to read even headlines. Highest-paid workers on the grounds — eight dollars a day for ticket sellers and six for payout cashiers — they were reviewing their unfamiliar assignments.

They were to put on a real ding-dong performance. You can still see something similar to early pari-mutuel machines on the quaint cable cars of San Francisco. When the conductor accepts a fare he reaches up and pulls a chain which rings a bell and causes the passenger count in an overhead viewing box to increase by one. Imagine the clang created by ten machines in a row, each machine equipped to tote up the tickets sold on eight horses. Each two-dollar ticket resulted in a vigorous pull, a vigorous clang and a grinding advance of one number in the overhead box. No secrets were possible. When the windows were closed the numbers were totalled, and when the winners came home all the money was paid out except for perhaps 5 percent kept by "the house." Nowadays the provincial government takes 5 percent, the federal takes .6 percent and 5.25 percent goes for purses, but the Edmonton track takes only 4.25 percent, tied with Calgary for lowest in North America.

In 1913 the delightful revenue possibilities of gambling and booze had not occurred to sober Canadian governments. In their maiden run the mutuel machines returned nearly 95 percent of the pot to the bettors and gave the exhibition a clear profit of $6,781.15. This compared neatly with $3,800 which would have been paid by the bookies and $10,500 received in grants from senior governments. A subtle change had occurred in the ten years since the Bulletin had defended racing purses because fast horses drew crowds to see prize exhibits of slow horses and fat cattle. By 1913 fast horses were not only attracting crowds; the money the crowds bet was important to financing the entire operation of "The Model Fairgrounds of the Dominion." That trend has never reversed.

Edmontonians were proud of all they saw on "The Model Fairgrounds," enjoying a glow produced in our own time by facilities developed for the Commonwealth Games. They found pride in the livestock pavilion, the grandstand, the manufacturers building, machinery hall, the barns, the dog building where five hundred canines could be judged at one time by an official named Mr. Barker. In raising this grandeur the association had achieved a funded debt of $430,000. The provincial government, in the same time span and with much superior resources, had been able to amass a debt of less than $23 million.

91

A trophy won at the Edmonton fair is shown with pride at Stony Plain.

Edmonton's city auditor, like any citizen, was proud of the figures and proud of the model fairgrounds, but he was also uneasy. He had doubts and fears about the arrangement between the exhibition board and the city — which had borrowed the $430,000. Ordinary people could understand the agreement but it was so informal he feared that lawyers and judges would not, and might contend that nothing had been done legally.

So the two parties engaged a lawyer to spell out their understanding in legal niceties. The city would lease to the association the land and improvements — and what improvements they were — for a dollar a year. Because of the city's financial commitment it would appoint thirteen of twenty-five directors, twelve to be elected by the shareholders. And the lessee would be bound to certain safeguards such as:

"The association will not carry on offensive trade."

A formal agreement, full of such phrases pleasing to the legally-tuned ear, came into effect January 1 1915, and although revised at five and ten year intervals ever since, the principle evolved in Edmonton's years of youthful exuberance has endured. The site acquired in the yeasty years 1906-14 has endured. Even the buildings endured till only yesterday. The young people of the boom builded with the careless rapture of Roman chariot drivers — but they builded well, better than they knew.

𝒯he 𝒜uman 𝒻actor

My Aunt Mary Adele Gorman was introduced to this term while attending the University of Chicago. She was one of the first Edmonton girls to reach higher education. One day a learned professor was trying to rationalize how a fine scheme of his had come to frustration. After ponderous thought he turned sadly to the wall and lamented: "Oh, the human factor!"

In their attempts to make the Edmonton Exhibition the greatest show on earth the directors of the first boomtime were often victims of the human factor. To cite just one example, the pain they suffered from Walter Sporle is documented in several entries from the minutes of their meetings:

September 12 1910
Moved by Grierson-Robertson that the Sporle stock farm be prohibited from showing for one year for endeavoring to show a grade stallion in a registered class. Carried.

December 19 1910
Moved by West-Robertson that W. Sporle be given a certain time to explain history of his horse in the registered class. Carried.

January 16 1911
Letter from W. Sporle was read re stallion "Romeo." Moved by Auld-West that the secretary be instructed to write to the American Percheron Society and ascertain if this horse is registered.

February 6 1911
Letters were read from the secretaries of the American Percheron Society and the American Breeders Percheron Registry Co. stating that no horse named "Romeo" is registered either in the French or American stud book.
Moved by Stewart-Grierson that Mr. Sporle be sent a copy of these letters and asked to appear before the directors on March 6.

March 20 1911
It was moved by Manson-West that the motion of September 12th be rescinded, provided prize money and ribbons won by the horse "Romeo" are returned.

July 13 1912
Walter Sporle signified his willingness to exhibit his stock provided that he was invited to do so. It was moved by Stewart-West that the communication be filed. Carried.

March 18 1914

A communication was read from Walter Sporle stating that he had not received a copy of the prize list for the spring show and asked that such be sent to him.

March 24 1914

A communication was received from City Solicitor Bown re the acceptance of Walter Sporle's entries . . . It was moved by Mr. Manson, seconded by Mr. Calder, that the manager send Mr. Sporle a prize list and write him saying that the association will accept his entries if he will write apologizing for the insulting language used to the manager respecting the Exhibition Association.

That's the book on Walter Sporle, but it's just volume one of a family saga. There was also Walter Sporle Junior, who accounted for the following entries in the official minutes:

August 17 1911

The protest of Walter Sporle Jr. re the Farmer Race, he claiming that the horses were not ridden by their bona fide owners was referred to the race committee with power to act.

April 27 1912

A letter from Walter Sporle Junior was read claiming second prize in the thoroughbred class at the spring show. It was moved by McGeorge-Colley that the prize be paid.

August 20 1913

A communication was read from Messrs. Emery, Newell, Ford, Bolton and Mount on behalf of Walter Sporle Jr. in connection with the Edmonton Futurity, being Race #8 on the program, and threatening that unless first and second money be paid to them instead of second and third, as awarded by the judges, that the matter would be taken into court.

September 7 1913

The manager reported that a writ had been served on him as representative of the Exhibition Association, on behalf of Walter Sporle Jr. for first and second money, instead of second and third, as awarded by the judges in the Edmonton Futurity. He also reported that the question had been taken up with the city solicitor, who had expressed his opinion that Mr. Sporle had no case.

Walter's case hung on the meaning of the word *trained*. The race was for horses foaled west of the Great Lakes in 1910 and trained in Canada. The clear winner was Benmore, owned by colorful Charlie Bremner, who once rode a horse into the stately Edmonton Club and on being instructed to apologize said he had already done so — to the horse. Walter's entries, Cyclone and Cylla Man, came trailing after "on a track better suited to boats" as the Journal put it, but Walter then claimed that Benmore was not eligible. He'd been sent to Couer d'Alene, Idaho, for two months of his young life and had therefore broken training. *Trained in Canada* meant literally that; a horse which had vacationed in Idaho was not wholly trained in Canada. The stewards said the argument was stupid and the city solicitor agreed, but on November 6 Walter took it to Justice Beck — whose ruling the next entry makes poignantly clear:

November 25 1913

City solicitor Bown was heard respecting the decision in the Sporle suit. He advised that the association appeal it, believing that there were good grounds for winning, and also to settle the question as to the control which the association had over matters of this kind.

While the wheels of justice turned in their calm unhurried circles, Sporle the Younger had a complaint about the Spring Horse Show of 1914:

May 20 1914

A communication was read from Walter Sporle Jr. claiming more prize money than he had been paid. The records for the classes in question, # 7 and #265, were produced and found to conform to the prize money as already paid to Mr. Sporle. Dwyer-McGeorge — that the decision of the judges as shown by the records in the office be sustained and that Mr. Sporle be notified that he has no further prize money due him.

October 21 1914

A communication was read from the association's solicitors in connection with the Walter Sporle Jr. suit for prize money at the spring horse show of 1914, stating that the President and manager had settled the same for $25.

Then comes the final entry in the drama of the Edmonton Futurity.

November 18 1914

The manager presented the decision given in the appeal of the suit brought by Walter Sporle Jr. against the Edmonton Exhibition Association, and in which the judgement in favor of the plaintiff for $950 with costs and interest since November 1913 was confirmed.

15 War and Bust

By the time the high court settled the matter, all the factors in the human condition had boiled up and exploded to create the First World War. The booster spirit, which had made Edmonton's square mileage second only to Chicago's, suffered quick deflation. Only five weeks after the armies marched the exhibition was driven to "A Retrenchment Plan to save $6,267." Among other economies, popular grounds superintendent Dave Stewart was let go and manager Stark had to move into Stewart's cottage.

The capitalists who had been lavishing on Edmonton packing plants and brick buildings, and subdivisions with poetic names, suddenly disappeared. About the only foreign entrepeneur who retained faith in the city was Lynn Welcher of Brooklyn, New York, who favoured us with a roller coaster and tunnel of love.

Mr. Welcher's amusements went up in 1915 along the south fence, half on the exhibition grounds, half in Borden Park. During fair week the association got 15 percent of the gross, which was welcome. By 1916, when total revenues dropped to $68,000, $481 came from thrill seekers who paid to experience the sharp dips and turns of the permanent roller coaster, and couples who floated through the dark passages of the tunnel on magnetically pulled boats, to cling to each other in fear when ghosts and skeletons loomed out of the Stygian void.

The tunnel of love was called The Old Mill. This was to avoid conflict with people of puritan sensibility. However, the roller coaster brought the exhibition board into conflict with the army. The soldiers were using it for an obstacle course, with resultant scar of boot and bayonet, and Ottawa was reluctant to finance repairs.

Early in 1915 the military and the exhibition made an informal joint housekeeping arrangement on the grounds. Sword and ploughshare lay side by side. While the exhibition carried on its own work the site was transformed into a basic training camp. Many of the horse barns were converted to barracks. A floor was put in the feed storage barn to create the Tipperary Theatre. Trenches were dug in the race track infield. On winter days recruits drilled in the arena. When a battalion was in training the army paid a dollar a day for maintenance, and eventually the association's single maintenance man was allowed to keep the dollar himself.

The 49th Battalion was first to occupy the barns and open spaces, and although the association appreciated the snap and panache the soldiers gave the Spring Horse Show it declined to contribute to Major Griesbach's fund to buy four machine guns for the unit.

When the 49th left for France it was followed on to the grounds by the 51st, the 66th, the 138th, the 194th, the 202nd "Sportsman's Battalion", the 218th. Row on row, the battalions formed, trained, and went to war, and as each paraded downtown to the trains the population of young and vigorous dwindled a further six hundred.

War comes to the Exhibition Grounds. Men of the 66th Battalion choose the Manufacturers Building as a backdrop for a group photo. On the stage in front of the grandstand a girl in the uniform of a Red Cross nurse pours out a patriotic song.

Every area of society responded to the challenge of the new-style war, none more quickly than that narrow sector which set off giant fireworks to conclude grandstand shows. The display of rockets and blazing forts and gunpowder booms and bombs bursting in air which had thrilled Edmonton fairgoers as Lord Baden-Powell's South African Relief Train and Lord Nelson's Shelling of Alexandria became the Bombardment of the Dardanelles.

Though the war fronts were explosive, life on the home front in Edmonton was slowing down to a pace that would hold until after the next world war. No longer bothered by growth the exhibition association settled in to the task of operating the facilities they had, year after year after year. But a lively summer fair was just as important to a static community as it was to a city in a state of boom. The board sought to involve key elements of the community in the life of the exhibition. In 1915 twenty-three associate directors were added.

Women were now recognized as a dynamic force. They voted on Edmonton money bylaws if they held property and the provincial government was soon to extend the franchise to them. Four groups were recognized: the Alberta Branch of the Women's Art Association of Canada (Mrs. D. Davies), Edmonton Handicraft Guild (Mrs. Archibald), Edmonton Consumers League (Mrs. A. N. Mouat), and the Women's Press Club (Mrs. Gerald O'Connor followed by Nellie McClung). Also included were the Edmonton Horticultural Society with which the exhibition joined to put on the flower show that year, the United Farmers of Alberta, the four provincial breeders associations sponsored by the exhibition, the Edmonton Trades and Labor Council, Board of Trade, Industrial Association and Produce Merchants Association, the Poultry and Pet Stock Association, Edmonton's two rival kennel clubs, the university, school board and technical school, Driving Club (horses of course), Jockey Club, and the Edmonton Golf and Country Club.

That was a rollcall of vital forces in the community, a small city whose growth had been stopped by war and whose population would not reach 100,000 till another war. The importance of involving all forces in the fair was obvious to the board. One means of achieving this was a pushball. The pushball had all other athletic artifacts beat for size, and for hilarity — a leather ball which blew up to a full diameter of six feet. Teams representing rival organizations commercial and social would face each other and swipe at the bounding monster until they huffed it and puffed it across a goal line. Pushball contests were a lively addition to events on the grounds, so popular that Manager Stark found it could be rented for fifty dollars a contest, and when Calgary fair promoters tried to borrow it were advised they could pay the regular price.

By 1916 the grim austerity of war was causing the board to seek means of livening the product. They came up with an inspired slogan: SELL YOUR HAMMER AND BUY A HORN. A real blockbuster that! A bit obscure now but all understood that good citizens ought to forego work for a short while, lay down their hammers and toot the horn of a good cheer and civic pride. To boost the level of levity manager Stark was authorized to engage the Presbyterian Quartette for the grandstand at eighty dollars, a hundred if necessary. A wartime shortage of rail cars forced a rescheduling of fair days. Edmonton's fair moved into July where it has remained ever since, and the "Glorious Twelfth" fell during fair week. Members of the Orange Lodge were persuaded to make their annual procession in honor of King Billy an exhibition parade. All these were attractions to be sure but a government ban on fireworks displays led the board to hire the best of all.

Blasting powder was needed for real battles and spectacles commemorating Lord Nelson's shelling of Alexandria became casualties of war. So the board took the 16 hundred dollars in the fireworks budget and hired the American girl aviator,

The Exhibition board didn't think Katherine Stinson was a spy.

Katherine Stinson, to ship her Curtiss biplane by train and put on two shows a day, flying off the racetrack infield and stunting past the packed grandstand. She also performed at the Calgary fair. The young lady was tiny and vivacious, a hit in the air and on the ground. When the week was over she went home to Texas where she and her brothers trained allied airmen, and the war dragged on.

Although Edmonton was far from the fighting fronts a certain number of residents helped prosecute the war by watching for German spies. Their vigilance affected the exhibition. They decided that Ivan Kircoff, a handyman who found occasional employment on the grounds, was really a German and therefore a spy. The board felt obliged to make Ivan prove he'd been born in the Ukraine as he claimed. But when the spy-hunters accused Katherine Stinson that was just too much. On November 8 1916, for the first and only time the board dealt with a resolution concerning German spies. They voted complete confidence in the loyalty of their charming guest, and received a nice note of appreciation.

The directors, regular and associate, were pleased with the year, and the surplus of $4,000. So were the provincial breeder associations which had headquarters in the Exhibition office. At the spring show 559 show animals were stabled and 87 bulls were sold, up from 23 the year before. During the fair there had been 1339 animals in the show rings, the most ever. The next year was even better and the *Norwest Farmer* of Winnipeg picked the swine exhibit for special praise.

> "The hog show held at Edmonton this year was the largest ever held in Alberta. It is no exaggeration to say that it was the greatest show of hogs ever seen in Alberta. It was exactly that and pronounced by Professor J. W. Elliott who has judged hogs at western fairs as the best lot of show hogs he has ever passed on in the west."

The praise of Norwest Farmer was a little repetitive but the boosters couldn't hear enough. They were cheered by other events of 1917.

A decorated car parade organized for the spring horse show by the Edmonton Automobile Club, 250 strong, was described as "the greatest collection of buzz-wagons ever seen in the capital city." And in the women's division of the summer fair prize money was increased to $61 to include a new class — Ukrainian handwork.

By 1918 government regulation took even more fun out of the fair. First fireworks, now — but let the Journal describe it:

> *July 9 1918*
>
> Horse-racing — denatured of betting by order of the Dominion Government for the duration of the war — was served up for edification of Edmonton racegoers yesterday. There were no deaths from heart failure. It is quite clear that horse-racing devoid of the pari-mutuels has no interest for the public. What though the horses be well-matched, and the races vigorous, they command no attention. As a result, the public watched the other grandstand displays with great interest, but ignored the horses. The gee-gees might as well have been running for 'Sweeney'.

Strong countermeasures were needed lest the entire fair be conducted for the mysterious Sweeney. A new slogan was devised, and though it lacked the imperative thrust of SELL YOUR HAMMER AND BUY A HORN it had the compensation of permanence. WHERE CITY AND COUNTRY MEET endured for half a century. The United Commercial Travelers did their best to dramatize the new theme. Travelling salesmen were pioneering the automobile on country roads built for wagons. They undertook to brighten Citizens Day with a parade of decorated cars from all over northern Alberta. The McFarland Shoe Company disguised their salesman's car to resemble one of the sample left shoes with which he toured the country. Henderson Signs made their car a battleship. Johnstone Walker's delivery van appeared as it does across the page. Some seven hundred automobile owners answered the call of the U.C.T. on Citizens Day, and every day high-speed autos entertained the crowds. The race track, which had once been denied to Barney Oilfield, king of auto racers, was opened to six speed demons who churned up clouds of dust to divert the crowds. For $350 the board hired a girl parachute jumper named Lucille Belmont, whose act was going up in a balloon and leaping gracefully to the infield. Lucille landed out on 118th Avenue on her first jump and cancelled the rest of her engagement, but there was no disappointment with the star attraction of 1918. In fact, through the long summer afternoon of July 9, as the Journal printed its gloomy assessment of horse racing denatured of betting, the crowd patiently held positions in the grandstand awaiting the triumphant return of their favorite, Katherine Stinson.

acing denatured of betting needed some spice. It was hoped that a harness race with mules might lp. Decorated automobiles were another brightener.

In 1916 Miss Stinson's aeroplane had been assembled on the exhibition grounds, but there had been two years' progress in aviation, spurred by needs of war and now she was going to fly all the way from Calgary. At twelve noon she would lift off the southern fairground; about half-past-two she would complete the first Calgary-Edmonton flight by touching down in front of the northern grandstand.

She took off on schedule but near Airdrie the plane's engine failed. She had to land in a farm field, walk to a telephone, and bring her mechanic out from Calgary. It was after five o'clock, when the journey could be resumed. She flew back to circle the starting point, and then headed north again, following the CPR track. Along the line station agents watched the buzzing biplane go overhead, then rushed inside and sent telegrams to her destination. Each was read to cheers of the crowd. Balzac. Airdrie. Crossfield. Carstairs. Didsbury. Olds. Bowden. Innisfail. Penhold. Red Deer. Blackfalds. Lacombe. Morningside. She was well ahead of schedule. In two hours she was making a trip that took two days by car. The telegrams kept coming. Ponoka. Wetaskiwin. Millet. Leduc. And then there she was, circling the grounds and coming in to land.

It was exactly 8:03 p.m. Among the crowd who raced to meet her was George Armstrong, the postmaster. Katherine had a post office sack with 259 letters put aboard in Calgary. Popular Katherine Stinson had just made the first air mail flight in western Canada. All for the fun of the fair. Manager Stark stood centre as the Postmaster took the historic bag.

6 *Peace and Plenty*

The armistice brought a fleeting illusion that the good old days of pre-war boom were reviving. Returning soldiers were back on the streets, and though not so young or so optimistic as before they were keen for a good time and had money — for a one-season fling anyway. For those involved in the exhibition the illusion was heightened by the demonstrable fact that the bounds of the grounds were being wider and wider set. Borden Park, eighty acres, was added to the site and the association set out to make it an amusement park, a miniature Coney Island. To the roller coaster and tunnel of love was added a merry-go-round, which operated two days a week. And plans for the present Borden Park swimming pool were made at this time, to be part of the complex. There was confusion over who had control of what — the city would lease the arena for hockey and then inform the association — and most of the Borden Park annex eventually went back to the city, but before it did the association put up the last major structure until after the next war, in which it served as an RCAF officers' mess. Provincial architect R. P. Blakey, co-designer of the legislative dome, did drawings for "a modern Women's Building — the only one of its kind in Canada."

The drabness of war had given fairgoers a pent-up appetite for sparkle and zest, and to add these ingredients to the Spring Show the board welcomed an attraction once turned away with contempt. Guy Weadick, founder of the Calgary Stampede, was paid $700 to put on a display of roping, whooping and hollering twice a day and this must have been good for Guy's morale since the Stampede was not yet respectable in its home town, and operated by itself in the off-season. A record 208 bulls were sold at the show, which was good for the morale of all.

The Western Canada Trapshooting Tournament "was also given ample room, with every safety provided for spectators, the shooting taking place over the lake section."

When summer came the Western Fairs Association teamed to bring one of the top grandstand attractions in the world — the military band of John Philip Sousa. "Observers noted more middle-aged spectators in the grandstand in proportion to the younger folks in attendance," said the annual report, "showing that those who do not care for vaudeville will attend ..." Attendance hit a record 111,710 — some tented in Borden Park, "the former Borden Park" said the annual report. And Sousa's band was not the only attraction. The association had its own airplane with combat pilots of the recent war to fly it.

"A Modern Women's Building — the only one of its kind in Canada."

The aircraft, a Curtiss JN-4 "Jenny" had been presented to the city of Edmonton by aviation prophet A. B. Carruthers, magnate of the Lake of the Woods Milling Company and developer of Edmonton's Glenora subdivision. With no airport or hangar the city leased it to the exhibition association and among the pilots was "Wop" May, local boy who had figured in the last fight of Germany's Red Baron. One afternoon May and his partner George Gorman gave the crowd extra thrills, diving at the bandstand where John Philip Sousa was performing. They put on their amusing extra show until the great musician-composer walked off the stand vowing never to return until someone got those damfools out of the air.

"We present our report for 1919 with considerable and justifiable satisfaction," said the directors, — with reasonable hope of more the next time around. But in 1920 attendance dropped ten thousand as the pace of life flagged and the city and its institutions settled into a pattern of holding — and holding and holding and holding.

A photograph of the grounds taken in 1920 could still be used in 1950. And the motto of the exhibition had an ironic twist. For nearly forty years city and country would meet well inside the boundaries of the city.

7 The 1920s Slow Speed Ahead

After 1920 the exhibition association did not publish an annual report as such — just a financial statement which varied little from year to year, covering three main areas of expense: the cost of six days of April dedicated to the spring livestock show; six days of July which brought the summer fair; and administration. 1926 was a typical year. Cost was summarized in this manner:

Spring livestock show	$ 15,813.15
Summer exhibition	$ 83,962.88
Spring race meet (two days)	3,531.82
Administration (including)	
$11,116.68 for salaries)	15,555.82
Total	$118,863.67

The figures changed little from one year to the next and there was no reason why they should when nothing else changed. However, though life in Edmonton was dull in terms of building permits, in terms of pure living and the satisfaction of participating, it was just fine. Community leagues were starting in the city, and the association where town and country met was conducted in the same spirit. City and country not only met; they couldn't be untangled.

The manager of the exhibition was also secretary of the breeder associations whose membership was imbedded in the shareholder list of the Ex. City and country worked together for mutual advancement, as Percy Abbott explained, and who was better qualified than Percy to explain the economic interlock? Percy came out from Ontario early in the century, taught in country schools and became a city lawyer. He'd been an alderman and president of the Board of Trade. He belonged to the Edmonton Club and the Country Club. With the Ex he was director and president and when manager W. J. Stark died on an eastern livestock judging tour in 1927 Percy Abbott took the job of manager for fifteen years. At an annual meeting Percy explained the economics this way:

"Therefore, gentlemen, while we show a profit of only $24.68 on our spring show we must not regard it as a failure; our justification for continuing the show — and the justification of those who contributed $12,350 to enable us to put it on — lies in the better livestock on our farms, which in turn means better financial returns, and more money to spend on improved farm equipment and comforts for the home, and the ultimate outcome is reflected in better banking and business conditions, both throughout the country generally and in our city."

Perhaps Churchill could have stated it better but everybody knew what Percy meant because they were all in it together. Even the staff of the Ex were in it. After the fall wool show they acted as brokers for the fleecy stuff. One year they marketed $27,000 worth of wool on behalf of 317 growers.

Edmonton's Commercial Grads, world basketball queens, lead the Exhibition parade of 1924.

Everyone involved had a sense of progress. Examples were cited in the souvenir grandstand program of 1926, the year of the mammoth historical pageant. Take butter. Production of butter hadn't grown much but exports had taken off: one million pounds in 1922, three million-plus in 1925. And competitions at famous fairs certified progress. The Chicago fair was glamour capital of the world for grain growers. In 1920 the products of Alberta grain fields had taken ten prizes in Chicago; in 1925 they'd captured 43. Then there was livestock. Every member of the breeding associations dreamed of winning an award at the Royal Winter Fair in Toronto. In 1922 Alberta breeders took fifteen prizes and one championship; two years later they showed 75 prize winners and six champions. Though herds weren't increasing in numbers there was proof of progress in the prize list.

In the city of Edmonton there were no visible signs of *growth* but just the same all citizens had a feeling of *progress,* a feeling in which they were encouraged by visiting millionaires. Millionaires used to pass through by train en route to golf holidays at Jasper, and they always told newspaper reporters they were watching Edmonton's progress with keen interest. That is, all but John Jacob Astor the

Merchants who put floats in the parade were entitled to a little "hard sell."

Third. The reporters couldn't get him awake to find out if he was watching our progress with interest.

But what citizen could feel minor league when there was major league hockey in the building designed for horse shows? The big ice, 220 feet long, glittered with the skills of Duke Keats, Art Gagne, Joe Simpson, Eddie Shore, Barney Stanley, Dick Irvine and others who were spirited away eventually when the Western League was broken up to stock American arenas with instant National Hockey League teams.

When the arena was in construction doubts had been expressed about the quality of the roof, along with other components, but the roof held secure on many a wild night of hockey including that night in 1923 when the Edmonton Eskimos and Regina Capitals went into overtime to decide the western championship. It survived the roar 10 minutes and 25 seconds later when the arm of the goal judge shot heavenwards to signal that Duke Keats had drilled home a penalty shot and Edmonton was in the Stanley Cup final against Ottawa. (Which we lost).

The hockey season had to end March 15 so the building could be made ready for the spring horse show, and since there was no artificial ice until the late 1930's this was no deprivation. Then, in summer, another sporting attraction filled the Arena and filled citizens with the notion that Edmonton was a place of importance. Becoming totally involved in the fortunes of a basketball team made up of girl graduates from the local commercial high school might seem the action of a small town but this team was world champion.

Then there was our $600 dollar airport. The city spent $600 to chop two runways out of the bush (and leased the grazing rights to a farmer to keep the grass down) but it was the first municipal airport in Canada, an operating theatre for the bush pilots of the 1930s.

Every citizen felt lifted by the pilots and the world basketball champions; felt they were "putting Edmonton on the map." Edmonton was even on the map in every grocery store in the United States where Canada Dry Ginger Ale was sold. In deepest south, in farthest west, the pink map of Canada decorated the label, and clearly marked was the capital city of Alberta — where the second batch of Canada Dry was manufactured for sale on the 24th of May 1907.

The lads in the Edmonton Newsboys Band certainly felt they were on the cultural map. They got the feeling on a rainy windswept night in 1926 when the elements beat down with unwelcome vigor on the outdoor stage and a concert had to be moved into the Arena. On that night our newsboys were invited to share the program with the band of His Majesty's Coldstream Guards, the only time in their history, it was said, that the premier regimental band in the British Empire ever shared the stage.

The Coldstream Guards had come all the way from England to help celebrate an anniversary: the twenty-first birthday, or coming of age, of Alberta the province and Edmonton the city. Each evening the band played before the mammoth historical pageant, in which six hundred citizens of all ages participated in eighteen tableaux and dance numbers to dramatize the progress of Edmonton from the dimness of pre-history to the dazzling present.

One of the featured performers was Lotta Dempsey, who went on to a career in journalism and the editor's chair of Chatelaine. Lotta had the role of Miss Canada. Miss Edmonton was played by Aletha Orr, who made it to the London stage. The pageant opened with blare of trumpets and a welcome from Miss Edmonton — in a voice which had to carry to the top of the grandstand because microphones were still two years off in the bright future which waited Edmonton. To the welcome Lotta replied: "Miss Edmonton, in the name of Canada and her fair provinces I acknowledge this your welcome. With pride we recognize in Edmonton one of the brightest gems in the crown of our Canadian achievement ..." Then appeared Father Time, played by Frank Walker, bailiff from the court house, who had just the booming voice to conduct Miss Canada past the progress. The first tableau was an Indian camp in which the residents were played by John Blue, secretary of the chamber of commerce, and other businessmen. There were Indians in the neighborhood who might have participated, but perhaps they didn't care for the script. Such as: "Their great interest in life was to procure food and devour it and to subdue their enemies. If a campaign proved ...... successful the return was celebrated with a grand savage dance." Apparently that day's effort hadn't been because the chaps from the chamber didn't favor the crowd with a grand savage dance. The pageant moved on past fur traders, missionaries, railroad builders, Frank Oliver's first printing press, Klondikers, Mounted Police. "Splendidly equipped, fearless and resourceful, this great police force was ever the terror of evil-doers and bad Indians."

Johnny J. Jones brought the midway each summer. People en route to the roller coaster and Old Mill could stop for temperance refreshments.

The procession came at length to a tableau of September first 1905, showing the platform party at the inauguration of the province — down at the old exhibition grounds on Rossdale flat. Then in mammoth finale came the dancing girls, hundreds of them, all teenagers, all local, in a brightly-costumed mosaic of the countries represented in the new Canada. English girls, Irish, Belgian, Chinese, Japanese, Scotch, French, Dutch, U.S.A. girls, Italian, English (again) and Canadian. That's the list, from which there are some obvious omissions, but the establishment of the time had not yet accepted newcomers from northern and eastern Europe. Even the Japanese and French girls were played by girls with names from the British Isles. But the audience loved the spectacle, and the mammoth pageant moved to its triumphant close to the rhythm of an upright piano, pounded by Herbert G. Turner.

The pageant theme was carried to two other events of of the memorable week. An Old Timers Cabin was opened and the CNR presented a relic of pioneer achievement for permanent display on the grounds — Engine 103, which had pulled the first train into Edmonton back in 1905.

The next year some of the directors thought a Stampede would make a nice attraction. Down in Calgary Guy Weadick had made the Stampede not only successful but respectable — so much so that it had merged with the exhibition. Conceding the excitement of a wild west show the majority felt that another mammoth historical pageant was in order, considering that 1927 was to be celebrated as Diamond Jubilee of Canadian confederation with events across the country. And also that pageants involved the whole community. The 1927 show had a cast of one thousand on stage, 1.3 percent of the entire population, comparable to a later involvement in the Commonwealth Games. Evelyn Parkes the dancing teacher again choreographed routines around the coming of the French siegneurs and the death of General Wolfe, but this time H. G. Turner, the pianist, was given an orchestra to conduct.

While the chaperones marshalled and costumed the young performers, people in the grandstand were already getting a full fifty cents worth. The show started at seven with a livestock parade led by the glamor boy of the barns, a prize shorthorn bull named King of the Fairies. Then came a half-hour vaudeville show. Then a forty-minute concert by the Australian National Band, and only then the mammoth pageant. Said the Journal: "The crowd received in spellbound silence the glittering kaleidoscope of the portrayal of the last three centuries of the Dominion's upwards struggles along the rough road to nationhood." The grand finale was grand indeed — 106 kids on stage in a "living flag" and among them was Noel MacDonald, who went on to fame as captain of the Commercial Grads. Of such an extravaganza one could not necessarily say: "That's entertainment!" but one could certainly state "That's involvement!"

In 1929 the exhibition came to its own occasion for historical pageantry, and with the original cast. Well, not all the original cast, but a sturdy dozen pioneers who remembered that far-off fair of fifty years ago at vanished Fort Edmonton. They were featured in the parade, the biggest ever and the longest too. "Took a half hour to pass," said the Journal.

The signal for the parade to start was a whistle blast from Trudeau's cleaning plant, on 103rd Street just south of Jasper. On other days the whistle blew at noon, Edmonton's downtown time signal, but on parade day it sounded at one p.m. In 1929 this brought the first flypast — a formation flight of biplanes from the Edmonton Flying Club. The band of the Princess Patricia's Canadian Light Infantry led off the procession while eight other bands — including those from Viking and Hay Lakes — waited their turns. Among decorated trucks and cars the place of honor went to a wagon driven by Pete Campbell, who had driven the Edmonton-

EDMONTON EXHIBITION

JULY 15 to 20 1929
50th. ANNIVERSARY
FIRST SHOW HELD 1879

N. FRANK OLIVER P.C.

| OPENING CEREMONY WILL BE PERFORMED ON MONDAY JULY 15. AT 8 P.M. BY THE HON. FRANK OLIVER P.C. | MAMMOTH PARADE THROUGH PRINCIPAL ~ STREETS TO ~ EXHIBITION GROUNDS at MID-DAY, MONDAY JULY 15. |

GRAND PAGEANT
ARABIAN NIGHTS
EVERY EVENING IN FRONT OF GRAND STAND

ALL THE MYSTERY AND GLAMOUR OF THE EAST BEAUTIFUL GIRLS EXOTIC DANCES

ALLURING MUSIC

Calgary mail stage back in 1879. As passengers Pete had Alfred Arcand in the Mounted Police uniform he had worn to the first fair, Jim McDonald, Tom O'Dell, Charlie Ross, and the other Rosses, Bill and Walter. And four ladies: Mrs. Leslie Wood, Mrs. Harrison, Mrs. Bill Howey and Mrs. Belcher whose husband had been a director of the first Agricultural Society.

That night, at the grandstand, the doughtiest survivor of all was on stage to declare the anniversary show open. Frank Oliver, publisher of the Bulletin, recalled highlights of 1879, including the fact that he was the correspondent who sent the story to the Saskatchewan Herald. It was Frank who telegraphed the historic message: "The first exhibition of the Edmonton Agricultural Society was held at Edmonton House on the 15th October." Then followed another pageant, though not historical this time. The directors decided that the death of General Wolfe had lost its appeal and elected instead for the Arabian Nights with the cast of a thousand "all appareled in the gay raiment of the exotic east." Again Evelyn Parkes arranged the dances, and Mr. Turner and Helen Barclay the music.

Fair week brought a sense of civic well-being. The fact of no change at the grounds (as in the city) could also be taken as an indication of permanence, which was no small comfort. The exhibitors at the Manufacturers Building felt it keenly. Each July the same men arrived with the same civic pride to decorate the same booths with their hams and cigars and teas and radio kits and fur coats. Department stores previewed fall fashions and Ogilvie Flour Mills put on a style show too. In addition to sacks of flour were dresses and shirts and blouses sewn from the empties. Most exhibitors had waged their own personal stakes to show the world they could build a new community of city-and-country in the far northwest and fair week was proof they hadn't failed. Though their building did not expand its wooden silhouette, on nights of the fair the familiar outlines glowed with white bulbs, in a radiance visible for blocks. No change at the Manufacturers Building. No change at the Arena. No change at the grandstand, even though the directors thought it would be nice to start the next fifty years with a new grandstand. A money bylaw went to the ratepayers in the fall of 1929, but they voted "No" and it stood for another twenty years.

Down But Not Out

Defeat was not surprising. The grandstand question was put to the ratepayers as the optimism of the roaring twenties collapsed with the stock market.

"We do not stand alone as an undertaking losing money in 1930," said Charlie Batson, president, reporting to the annual meeting of the exhibition. But if company is comfort for misery, 93 percent of Class A fairs in North America lost money in that first year of depression and Charlie was undismayed. "The association must carry on," he declared. "Our success is not measured by our profits or losses but by the benefits our work contributes to the agricultural life."

The business life of Edmonton was firmly meshed in the farm life of the countryside. The exhibition's theme of city and country meeting was observed in the heart of the city. A guest at the Macdonald Hotel could see it with a short walk. After lunch at the Edmonton Club — which had been taken over by the city for unpaid taxes but was encouraged to operate because the city needed the club for prestige — he could stroll to the farmers' market, on the square where the Centennial Library now stands. The farmers' market was a real slice of country. Off the northeast corner was the city hall — now refaced as police headquarters. Off the southwest corner was the city's prestige office building, the McLeod Block. Percy Abbott, manager of the exhibition association, had his law office up there on the seventh floor, and conducted much fair business among legal considerations. When country and city met, the population of the country outnumbered the city two to one, just the opposite today. The maxim that "when the farmer has money everybody has money" was still economic fact. The farmer had no money.

In fair week, mammoth grandstand pageants became memories of the prosperous faroff twenties, for even with a thousand unpaid performers donating their time the expense was beyond budget. In mammoth times professional acts had warmed up the audience for the pageant. Now the audience had to warm themselves for the professionals. They were invited to Come and Sing Your Blues Away, with community singing led by Reverend Mr. Stone, the Baptist minister. Even the grounds shrank as the city took back Borden Park, but President Charlie pulled glad tidings out of his hat for the annual meeting which closed out dark and dreary 1931. He spoke of profits. The events of the year had shown profits, small but with honor. Only when cost of administration was counted — at the insistence perhaps of killjoy auditors — did the year's operation show a loss of $14,800.22.

Charlie's fiscal fantasy was a form of "beating the depression" and no one took it too seriously or questioned the immense value of the $15,000 spent on administration. $11,000 went for salaries; to general manager Percy Abbott, to groundskeeper John McGaffin, and to the office staff, working away under the seats in a corner of the Arena. Louise Holmes the secretary had been in the office since 1912; Alex Bonneau the chief clerk since 1914; and Marjorie Hunter since 1925.

This experienced trio served not only the exhibition but the four breeder associations as well; handling their letters, their accounts, their creditors, their complaints, and their conventions, mostly at city hall. The mayor of Edmonton was proud and pleased that city and country should meet in the council chamber, a quaint room still adorned with brass spitoons of a colorful past. The team of Holmes, Bonneau and Hunter also served the Shorthorn Club, acted as brokers and bankers for the annual bull sale, the annual wool sale, and following the poultry show helped produce an exciting statistic of 1931: seventy-five carloads of turkeys were exported from Alberta that year. And speaking of turkeys they had to put up with jokes full of economic good cheer. "What's the strongest animal? The pig because it can lift the mortgage on a farm." And they had to be diplomats. An exhibitor showing a prize mortgage lifter could be difficult as a stage mother showing a prize child in a tapdancing competition.

There was no danger that the cost of administration would be construed as bad news, and Charlie had some genuine good news about 1931. News about the races. As a name attraction for Citizens Day that year the race committee had brought in the great Johnny Longden, and four of the winners of his fabulous career were booted home to Edmonton cheers. But in darkest depression all race horses were beginning to look like winners to those trying to preserve the exhibition. With gate and concession money credited to general revenue the horses still returned a profit of $2,300. Handsome, said Charlie.

And the arrangement was mutually handsome, because racing and the exhibition needed each other. Without the connection the sport of kings would have died on the prairies. That's the opinion of those who ought to know.

There are many, of course, who would consider the demise desirable. Some objectors oppose gambling on principle. Others feel that racing does not promote the educational objectives for which the association is subsidized by grants, tax advantages and use of city-owned land. They argue that the emphasis given to racing, crowds out these objectives. Though racing abounds with opportunity for argument the purpose of this chronicle is not to settle arguments but set them forth. Set them forth and provide facts which debaters may employ as they deem useful. But it's a fact that the exhibition drifted into two major activities without ever making a premeditated decision to do so. One activity is racing, the other is big-sport-and-show-business.

Take sport first. This activity stemmed from having the biggest barn in town. Early in the century the Edmonton fair — along with those in Calgary, Lethbridge, Medicine Hat, Moose Jaw, Regina and Saskatoon — was roped into sport. Put up the biggest barn in town in aid of agriculture and the world will beat a path to your door with schemes for hockey leagues, skating carnivals and big events in general. In two world wars the Canadian government hired Edmonton's big barn for military training and our brickpile was certainly more impressive than Calgary's Victoria Arena, a shaky wooden box which somehow failed to burn down until workmen demolishing it years later accidentally set the place on fire.

Without the brick barn where would Edmonton have held the events which loomed so important in depression's dark night? Where, for example, would they have held the biggest single occasion of the era, the reception for Lord Baden-Powell, founder of the Boy Scouts, whose military campaigns had once been celebrated in firework scenes at the fair on Rossdale flat? That was a night to remember. As proud parents and aunts jammed the seats, the scouts, guides, brownies and wolf cubs of Northern Alberta marched into the arena, past their beaming founder, while the band of the 49th Battalion played the longest rendition of Colonel Bogey in history.

Through depression's dark night the Manufacturers Building glows with optimism.

In summer a basketball floor was put down on the wood shavings on which the Commercial Grads, greatest women's basketball team in the world, outshot all challengers. In winter came the Glenora carnival. Members of the Glenora Skating and Tennis Club spent months working on routines and costumes for a weeklong ice show which was enjoyed by the whole community. Though the Arena was a long jaunt away on the streetcar, Edmonton had no place else. Then there was hockey, junior games on Sunday afternoons where one could cheer a choice of favorites: The Edmonton Athletic Club, the Maple Leafs or the South Side. And on week nights two senior teams competed in leagues with Calgary. One could cheer for the Dominions, who advertised Dominion Motors, or the Soops. The Soops were the Superiors, sponsored by Gainer's packing plant, one of the booster firms which bid up the prices on blue ribbon steers. Winter was shorter then because the Arena didn't boast an artifical ice plant. Calgarians could boast of manufactured ice in Victoria Arena — and did they ever.

In the 1940s Edmonton even got into cultural entertainment when a new livestock sales pavilion was recognized as the biggest available concert hall for Nelson Eddy, his singing screen sweetheart Jeanette Macdonald, and the Minneapolis Symphony. After sixty years of big barn syndrome the exhibition association hauled off and built the Coliseum. A big, big activity, and it was never planned. It just happened, and it just growed — like Topsy.

115

Fairs throughout North America have sport facilities — CNE stadium is home to the hopeless Argos and hapless Blue Jays. However, a connection with racing is almost unique to Alberta and Saskatchewan. The alliance is found in London, Ontario, and Omaha where racing is part of the Nebraska State Fair. Elsewhere the horses run for private enterprise. Even Winnipeg, where racing started with the fair, went private in 1925. The Edmonton exhibition (like those in Calgary, Regina and Saskatoon) got into racing in the nineteenth century. The sport of kings was the natural competition of the frontier, racing added fun to the fair, and there was stabling for livestock. The pony connection was never a deliberate strategy. It just started and it just growed. Heavens, how it growed. In 1931 the mutuels handled $187,000 for six days of thoroughbreds. In 1978 the track resounded to 77 days of thoroughbreds and 79 days of standardbreds engaged in harness racing. The mutuels processed $48 million, of which the exhibition kept three million — enough to carry the debt on the Coliseum.

After a hundred years of effort the most visible signs of the exhibition — visible for miles in the right directions — are the Northlands Coliseum and grandstand. The structures, and the historic facts on which they rest, will strike citizens in different ways depending on how they respond to the following questions:

    (a) Is racing necessary?
    (b) Is the Coliseum necessary?
    (c) Is the exhibition necessary?

By 1979 the once-clear consensus in the community about the role and methods of the association was lost in the welter of progress. A long and probing public debate will be necessary to regain that consensus, though it can never again be as simple and neat as it was in 1932 when "city and country met."

The meeting was profitable that year, $10,000 to the good, fourth highest among Class A fairs in North America, despite the depression, despite deducting the cost of administration.

Success was a selling job. The boosters went out to sell "rain insurance", that is, advance tickets. Rain was ever the critical unknown in the success of outdoor events. The Duke of York Chapter, Imperial Order Daughters of the Empire, pushed advance sales for the spring show. The Canadian Legion sold tickets for the summer fair in the towns of northern Alberta and placed $9,484 in the bank before opening day.

Despite all, 1932 was a success, and bold measures were taken to boost 1933. The Spring show was reduced to three days and prizes were cut 75%, down to $2,000. That may seem a strange method of boosting but it discouraged "pot hunters," wealthy outsiders who shipped in sure winners for the prestige of a trophy with Edmonton engraved on it. So the prize money stayed home to boost the economy and the local packing plants showed their local pride by high bidding on the winners. Price-per-pound could be a vital statistic in community morale. If our champion sold on the hoof for as-much-per-pound as the winner at Chicago it meant we were in the same league as the windy city, even if we didn't have Al Capone and Machine-Gun Kelly. It just happened that president Jim Sutherland and manager Percy Abbott were in Chicago for the American Fair Managers meeting in the fall of '33 and were able to report a surplus of $12,837.52 on that depression-year operation. It further happened that the United States ended Prohibition that week giving full scope for celebration of good news.

Though 1934 was thought of as "the depth of the depression" friends of the exhibition found even more to celebrate. The staff shipped 83 tons of wool for the sheepgrowers. Prizes increased 20 percent. $24,000 was paid out in wages, and $15,618 went to the city's unemployed, given work by the events and by improve-

The Exhibition Association is not concerned exclusively with horses, cattle, sheep and swine. The raccoon is a resident of Borden Park Zoo. From 1925 to '37 the Ex sponsored the Edmonton Zoological Society.

ments to the grounds. Debt to city and bank were paid off and the association still came out $14,000 ahead.

Attendance was off a bit at the start of the 1935 fair. Just 20,209. But boosters were quick to point out that this was no sign of a faltering economy. The unemployed were admitted free and Unemployed Day had been moved from Monday to Thursday. However, the big one was Tuesday — Parade Day. "20,000 WATCH PICTURESQUE PARADE," wrote the Journal. "It was the first exhibition parade in years, and the sidewalk watchers moved a vote of thanks to parade officials . . . Perhaps the most stupendous float in the parade was that of the Army and Navy store, which was done in the style of a huge ship and named SS Edmonton." The review also featured Mayor "Fighting Joe" Clarke in a cowboy hat, nine bands including the Stettler Elks band, and a leading formation of fourteen Mounted Policemen. And in the evening at the racetrack came FASCINATIONS OF 1935 — Super Grandstand Performance.

It was all so spectacular that president George Ball was moved to defend the association against "often-heard complaints that *attractions* are supplanting the agricultural purposes of the fair."

117

George Ball was a lift to the spirit at this time when spirits were sorely tried. His career was assurance that all would come out right in the end. George had arrived here in 1895 with a one-way ticket from Nebraska, assured by a CPR land agent that farming in pioneer Alberta would be an economic joy. (His bride Lova was to follow in a few months when she earned her own one-way ticket by teaching.) The Balls cleared a farm at Sherwood Park, though in the woods just beyond were cougars who coveted their hens and had to be sent packing with Lova's broom. Early in the century, just for fun, they entered a pig and a sheep at the fair on Rossdale flat and won two ribbons, a blue and a red, trophies so exciting that they were mounted on the wagon like pennants for the long drive home to Sherwood Park. George's interest and influence grew from this fair. Eventually he was national president of the sheepbreeders and swinebreeders and head of the provincial cattlemen. In 1931 a year if ever there was one for men of faith in the country to come forward, George and son Bob took sixty of their sheep and pigs on a tour of Canadian fairs and came riding home with 161 ribbons. When you talked to George Ball you sensed that everything would come out right — even the new crisis with Ottawa.

The rhubarb of '35 had a parallel with the present. Ottawa looked at our hard-earned surplus and was not pleased. Vowed the deputy minister of agriculture: Federal handouts will go only to fairs which are losing money — Edmonton's grant of $4,000 is in peril. However, Edmonton's mayor was not known as "Fighting Joe" for nothing. So the Feds want to help losers? Let's show them a loss. Let's change the accounting system. The books don't show the value of free rent of city land, or maintenance and improvements by the city, or a contribution to the sinking fund. Let's show our spirit. Let's show a bigger loss than anybody.

George and the boys were impressed. They couldn't do everything Fighting Joe proposed, but with the obvious help of the city comptroller, who was also auditor for the association, they performed some neat disappearing tricks. The comptroller was John Hodgson, that slyly humorous Lancashireman who served the city as financial wizard for some forty years. They depreciated every asset they could get away with to a value of a dollar. Loose tools, for example, an asset worth $60.15 in 1935, were worth a dollar a year later. These disappearing acts brought the 1936 surplus down to $9,000, and the federal grant, though reduced, declined only 25 percent.

In 1937 the surplus really was down, below $2,000 but no one was depressed. Two days of the fair were lost because of heavy rains, but few complained about that — not after years of the dust bowl. And the morale boost of a profit was no longer needed.

Prosperity had by no means returned, but the common opinion was that the depression was over, even though there hadn't been enough money to save old Engine 103. The historic steamer which pulled the first train into Edmonton had rusted and sprouted weeds and vermin and the health officer had declared it an unsanitary nuisance. $600 was too much to spend on relics when people were in need.

19 Hurry Hurry Hurry

If you went to the Sunday afternoon ball games at Renfrew Park you'll never forget the cheer that went up, a long swelling cheer that wasn't for heroics on the diamond. Even the players turned to look as the Royal American Shows midway train made its appearance on the High Level Bridge bringing the fun of the fair to Edmonton. Cars of the Royal American Special were painted in circus colors, in wild contrast to the drab reddish boxcars of regular trains. People brought up in today's expectations of entertainment will never comprehend the excitement which fair week brought to Edmonton, a city of eighty thousand, a city in which entertainment was a new movie on Saturday night, Sunday ball games and, in winter, Sunday afternoon junior hockey games at the Gardens.

The train would pass on out of sight and the game would resume but in the evening extra streetcars would carry a rush of families to the grounds. Hurry, hurry, hurry, to enjoy the magic of favorite rides and sideshows being bolted together and hoisted into position. No new thrills were expected. There was sufficient magic watching the familiar ferris wheel and merrygoround take shape and start to move in trial circles. And the show was absolutely free. Not till Monday noon could the kids hurry hurry hurry to spend the dimes and nickels and birthday dollars set aside to buy a portion of the fun of the fair. The exhibition brought a week of hurry hurry hurry to a scene in which hurry had little use the rest of the year. The snorting of engines which moved the rides and raucous enticements of the barkers made a rough agreeable music in the chronic stillness. Noise meant activity and activity was welcome. Noise was specialized, most interestingly in the building which housed the cat show — perhaps because it also housed the bird show. A confusion of things to do and see greeted the visitor, and those who were confused could consult Mrs. Parkhill. Mrs. Parkhill, a teacher at Norwood School, was a familiar personality — summer after summer at the information booth in front of the grandstand.

But after six days and nights of hurry hurry hurry the site was plunged again into silence. On the next Sunday morning the midway was a mute desolation of torn papers and wood shavings which carpeted the ground in lieu of pavement. During the night the ferris wheel and merrygoround and sideshows were unbolted and spirited away to Saskatoon. In the wake of the nocturnal exodus the only sound was of kids, kicking at the shavings, prospecting for fallen change. This writer well recalls the thrill of disturbing a clump of shavings and seeing the rim of a quarter project from the mud. Quarters in those days bore the head of King George V and packed real purchasing power. When summer flew by and the kids returned to school — and wrote their essays on the topic: "What I Did On My Vacation" — the exhibition, what else, loomed large. What else indeed? What else was there?

In 1936 the Ex made the grounds a showcase for a "Boost Alberta" project. The McMurray tarsands were honored. "A mile of walks" was laid, using the wonderguck on which Alberta pinned hopes of eventual prosperity and paved highways. However, the project did not reach the midway. There was still more money to be made kicking coins out of shavings than refining tarsands.

Next the Ex did something about the weather. Winter was made longer — with an artificial ice plant in the brick barn, and when Gainer's and Dominion Motors dropped the sponsorship of their hockey teams the Ex came to the rescue of senior hockey fans with a team called the Eskimos. To ensure victories over Olds, Drumheller, Calgary and Lethbridge, Mark Maveety was brought back from eastern exile at a yearly salary of $1,000, highest ever paid a local player. But the Eskimos spent the season being ground into the artificial ice in manner so dreadful that next year even the team name was changed, and the Edmonton Flyers, honoring our bush pilots, took the ice. To pilot the Flyers, sharpshooting centre Eddie O'Keefe was brought in, and to help attract Eddie the street railway provided a job driving a streetcar — with time off for games and practices.

O'Keefe's Flyers earned more applause than the Eskimos but the loudest, the longest, the most fevered cheers were for juniors — the great Edmonton Athletic Club teams which mowed down western opposition en route to national finals. With artificial ice all EAC home games could be played in Edmonton — even unto spring. Seventy-five hundred fans were allowed to squeeze into the brick barn, and if they couldn't find a place to stand could sit in the rafters and send the EAC against Wally Stanowski and the St. Boniface Seals on veritable waves of sound. Seventy-five hundred fans, nearly a tenth of the population. The barn must have been less flammable then. The fire marshal didn't object.

When time came to recall vacations of 1938, kids had a new experience to write about. Few had ever seen a large building under construction but that summer they were able to alternate between two — the new department stores of Eaton's and the Hudson's Bay Company, structures which made more impression on the kids than on the skyline. Out at the exhibition track, $300 was invested in new technology. The "eye in the sky" was the fast camera which settled arguments among people who had put "two dollars on the nose" as to which nose had emerged victorious. 1939 was a lovely summer. The night air pulsed with hit songs of the big bands. The exhibition spent more than $700 on decorations, and at the track a further $400 was invested in new technology — a starting gate. But sinister eyes glowered in the sky over Europe that summer, and the dogs of war snarled at the starting gate. Once again the fairgrounds were to become a military base. Kids who had so recently flocked to the grounds on children's day and gleaned fallen change from the shavings on the midway would be coming through the new 115th Avenue gate to join the Royal Canadian Air Force.

Children's Day at the grounds. Entries in a junior calf-feeding competition line up in front of the arena. In front of the grandstand manager Percy Abbott and Lieutenant Govenor J. C. Bowen make the draw for a prize bicycle. The tickets are in an old butter churn.

121

20 On Active Service

For a time the war seemed unreal, something heard on the radio, like music of the big bands. Young people appeared on the streets in uniform but seemed to have little connection with the conflict on the radio — news broadcasts from London preceded by chimes of Big Ben; speeches of Winston Churchill. An exhibition parade was held in 1940 but by another year the massive war effort of the small country was affecting every activity. The parade was cancelled for the duration — the directors consoled themselves with the thought that $2,000 was saved — and the ice plant went out of the Arena as the Air Force laid drill floors on the shavings. Floors and showers were installed in the livestock barns, the Manufacturers Building became an airmen's mess hall. Things of which there had been a surplus were suddenly in short supply. Sugar was rationed, gasoline was rationed, even boxcars. The Royal American midway, which had travelled with more than sixty cars, was allocated twelve and stayed home. A summer fair was held in 1942 with a small midway in Borden Park but then the fair itself disappeared as the facilities were fully occupied by young Canadians come to join the Air Force, and airmen arriving from Britain, Australia and New Zealand for the Commonwealth Air Training Plan. Only one "ride" remained on the grounds, the Link trainer, an earthbound airplane which tested the reflexes of recruits en route to flying schools.

In 1942 this writer took up temporary residence in one of the barns from which livestock had been evicted and began the life of a navigator guarding the Arena from sabotage. The brick barn was beyond the range of Axis bombers but was apparently a ripe target for saboteurs who were to be repelled with Ross rifles, though the rifles hadn't been fired in the lifetime of any of the recruits.

After a week or so the writer was transferred to the protection of the south fence, which had a fringe benefit. The Women's Building had been converted to an officers mess. When Jasper Park Lodge closed at the end of that summer the pastry cook had decided to enlist and in the still of the night would be at his stove doing his gorgeous stuff with the likes of lemon chiffon pie. Although his wares were intended for the officers he seemed to associate the recruits who guarded his kitchen with the students who had worked summers at the Lodge. Students were always hungry.

What had become of the exhibition association? The pastry chef didn't know. The Link trainer instructor didn't know. The padre didn't know, or give the matter a thought, but the association was still out there — holding a narrow strip along the tracks. With a lean-to barn, a few pens and a workshop converted to an office (and directors' meeting room) the association was carrying on. The strip lay between the Arena and the tracks, such a well-guarded secret that airmen sneaking in over the fence late at night would land in the remains of a stock show and find yet another fence to scale. Edmonton's mayor, John Fry, was anxious that the show go on: the spring livestock show and sale, the spring horse sale, the fall show and sale, the winter poultry show. In Winnipeg the "country" side of the exhibition had shut down in the first world war and never revived. So the show must go on, even though wartime demand created a shortage of locations, along with sugar, gasoline and boxcars. Any structure with roof or basement was required for some wartime purpose. The Empire Theatre (the Trocadero Ballroom) was converted to offices for an American firm working on the Alaska Highway. When Edmonton's turn came to host the provincial poultry show the association was grateful for the Palace Gardens, an east Jasper Avenue dance hall of such riotous reputation it was out of bounds to members of the Air Force.

The cluckfest was a show that must go on because agribusiness events were the war effort of the people in the association, their way of backing up the lads making the transition to military life by marching on their midway and patrolling their fences. Food was a weapon in Roosevelt's "arsenal of democracy." Armies, air forces, civilian populations at war — all moved on their stomachs. Those who held the 200 shares of the association felt their program was an important contribution and Charlie Wilson put it in words for all of them.

Charlie said it at an annual meeting in the council chamber of old city hall, at a low point in the fortunes of the allied cause, the night of December 28 1942. It was also a low point in the affairs of the association. Percy Abbott, the colorful dynamic manager, had died that year and Charlie, as president, was filling a dual role. Charlie was certainly right for the time. A Nova Scotian, he had come to Edmonton in 1903, been a shareholder since 1912, and represented both city and country — with a contracting business, and feedlots at his farm on the Namao Road. The program for 1943 was to be livestock shows only — on which but $13,000 would be spent.

No races to plan for, no midway, fun and games suspended "for the duration," War had returned the association to the condition of that first Edmonton Agricultural Society of 1879. But the founders had a sense of mission. So had the group who turned up at city hall on that bitter night of 1942, travelling over streets and country roads still banked with snows of the worst November blizzard.

Only the dedicated and durable turned up that night, and they were of such granite durability that some important names in the history of the association would also be answering the roll for centennial celebrations of 1979. Bill Muir for one. Bill wore a "city" sticker in the caucus where city and country met. He'd been recruited by Percy Abbott for a contribution to the cause, not money of course. "We had no money," says Bill, "all we had was fun." He was with Hook Signs, and had advice to give on advertising of events and decorating them too, and if his advice was deemed good was authorized to get out and do it himself. Bill's idea for brightening spring horse shows involved going out into the countryside with a Hook Sign truck, the Ex didn't have one, and crunching through the last snows of winter with an axe securing evergreen trees to pep up the drab interior of the Arena. Lee Williams, who succeeded Charlie Wilson as president, was another with the "city" sticker — a livestock commission agent at the North Edmonton stockyards, where city and country met in the strict economic sense. Lee had been recruited to contribute his knowledge to the economics of raising and selling. Any chap who voted one of the 200 shares was expected to make a contribution of special ability unpaid, unstinted, and though many things have changed that principle is still in effect. In 1978 one executive member attended some 300 exhibition meetings in addition to running his own business.

Roy Ballhorn made the longest drive to make his contribution to the annual meeting of 1942, steering through banked drifts all the way from Angus Ridge, near Wetaskiwin, where he'd left his concerned wife and unconcerned herd of prize beef cattle. Roy's special interest was the Aberdeen Angus — "Is there any other kind?" — and he was president of the provincial and Canadian cattlebreeders and offered his own prizes for junior exhibitors at fairs in Alberta and

B.C. In 1910, as a youth of eighteen he'd come to Edmonton for his first exhibition. In 1979 he would be in to help recall events between that event and the centennial.

Roy Marler also came in out of the cold that night — from Bremner. Roy is a member of Alberta's Agricultural Hall of Fame, his credentials including work with purebred hogs, as a farm economist and adviser to senior governments, and a term as president of the exhibition, with which he had his first contact in 1905. That event was made memorable by two souvenirs: a Waltham gold watch, which he found partly buried in the mud of the Rossdale fairground, and a white ribbon with a cigarette attached, a gift to all patrons from a tobacco company. Roy would have enjoyed sporting the cigarette at '79 centennial celebrations — if one of the Marler sons hadn't snitched it and smoked it in the long years between.

Although Roy Marler's memories predate the province of Alberta, no one at the centennial would out-remember Lawrence Rye, another president, noted for interest in Clydesdale work horses. Lawrence's first exhibition was way back in 1893, and he was no mere spectator. He handled the family's favorite shorthorn dairy cow, Butterfly by name, at a showring on 97th Street, site of today's city market. The judges thought Lawrence was too small to control Butterfly but he knew better. The previous summer, at age eight, he and an eighteen-year-old neighbor had hauled freight to Athabasca Landing with horses, and Lawrence had found going back to grade three a real bore after such excitement. Coming west with the famous Parry Sound Expedition (led by Tom Pearce who coined the name Sunny Alberta) he had nursed the hope that no schools would mar the promised sunshine. Lawrence Rye's exhibition memory, in centennial summer, would span an incredible eighty-six of the hundred years.

Lawrence drove in from Namao for the annual meeting of 1942. Two others, prominent on the "country" side, who answered the roll that night, didn't make the centennial but thanks to a strong family tradition in the association their sons would reminisce for them. J. W. Hosford, dairyman, breeder of prize Holsteins and member of the Agricultural Hall of Fame would be represented by W. J. Hosford. And the share of Henry George Cresswell, proud owner of Poppy, judged the best Clysdesdale mare in Canada, would be voted by George Henry Cresswell. Charlie Wilson didn't make it to centennial but son Lloyd had a term as president two decades later. In Charlie's term Lloyd was learning the basics by running errands for the directors and the two employees — Alex Bonneau the chief clerk, and Barbara Bannerman, who had become secretary when Louise Holmes retired.

Routine business accomplished on the night of December 28 1942, Charlie rose to tell the shareholders about their contribution to the Allied struggle. He was a forceful speaker if not stylish. One year he had nearly won the mayor's chair from Fighting Joe Clarke. In build he resembled Winston Churchill, and though Churchilll would have phrased Charlie's ideas with greater flourish, if the leader of the English speaking peoples could have been in the council chamber that night he'd have been chomping his cigar in vigorous approval. With pride and conviction Charlie reported:

"I am informed that the Edmonton district at the present time has the honor of being the greatest producer of bacon for Britain in the whole Dominion, and further that the meat packing industry in the city of Edmonton are processing more bacon for Britain than any other point in the Dominion, no small honor I assure you.

"I am one of those who believe that your association has played a part in bringing this about. Only a few years ago the type of hog raised and bred in this part of the country did not lend itself to produce the best bacon for the British market. But education supplied by the federal and provincial governments and our university have done much to better the type. Coupled with that education has been your association, where breeders could bring their product to a central place and compare it with others.

"I feel that if we can continue to keep our livestock at a high standard, when the war is over we will not only be shipping bacon to Britain but will be called upon to assist in supplying the war stricken countries with foundation breeding stock, not only in hogs but in cattle and horses as well."

There was more, but to an association seeking a meaning for existence, Charlie had already said it all.

21 1945-51 Towards a New Era

While war had come with a whimper, peace exploded with a bang. Germany surrendered on May 9 1945 and on July 10 the summer fair returned to Edmonton. And the crowds returned too. 176,000 went through the turnstiles — the most ever. Throngs returned to the racetrack too, and wagered so handsomely for six days that the association was enriched by $33,000. This raised an age-old controversy on which President Lee Williams was moved to comment: "There has been a certain amount of criticism as to the races but we must admit they have been profitable and to carry on the livestock events we have to have money . . . . ."

As life returned to easier styles of peace the Royal American midway operators were on the circuit again. Racehorse owners were back on the circuit. Livestock breeders were back on the circuit too, and there was one circuit for all. Carneymen, horsemen, stockmen. Inseparable components of a western fair, they moved together on their special trains and the stockmen felt they were the most important because horses, cattle, sheep and hogs were what fairs were all about. And the directors of the Edmonton exhibition association felt the same. Of twelve company-elected directors, six were farmers (compared to two of twelve in 1979).

For twenty-year-old Bill Hosford there was fun and satisfaction in riding the stock train again, renewing acquaintances going back to his first circuitous summer at age eight. The exhibitors were friends and competitors, boisterously friendly and fiercely competitive as the chaps who pitted racehorses against each other. Competition in the showring was spirited as on the oval track. Stockmen had their own colors, just like the racing fraternity, with which they painted their tack boxes and gear. Holstein fanciers, of course, favored patterns of black and white. Bill's dad had got caught up in the excitement of the showring after coming home from the first world war. He'd started dairying near Sherwood Park with four grade cows. Then he bought a purebred Holstein which gave as much milk as the four ordinary cows combined, and he just had to show off the winner and was soon on the circuit.

The railroads helped the cause. They'd rent a boxcar at half price for the entire season. Fifty to sixty cars of lowing, mooing, whinnying, baaing, oinking livestock, the pride of the prairies, would form at Brandon in late June, follow the rails to Calgary, Edmonton, Saskatoon, Regina, Great Falls, Billings, head over the mountains to Vancouver and then over the sea to Victoria on railroad ferries. The journey was a western epic, repeated each summer.

Friday was traditional moving day for the stock train, leaving the loading platforms clear for the carneymen and horsemen who were obliged to move on Sundays. Friday was hectic and colorful, splashed with sounds human and animal, as the pride of the farms were enticed aboard the cars. Like a reenactment of Noah's Ark the horsemen were cajoling their Clydesdales and Percherons, the dairymen their Holsteins, Jerseys and Ayrshires, the beefmen their Aberdeen Angus, Shorthorns and Herefords, the sheepmen their Oxford and Hampshire breeds, the hog fanciers their Yorkshires, Tamworths, Berkshires, Poland Chinas, Duroc Jerseys, and the newest breed, the Lacombes, a line founded in Canada.

Fifteen Holsteins chosen from the Hosford herd could ride in roomy comfort in one boxcar, while Bill and handler Lloyd Pickard and one or two hangers-on rode

A typical postwar racing crowd throngs the paddock area.

in a loft hung four feet from the roof. On one trip over the mountains the handlers were joined in the upper berth by four newborn calves which had joined the herd on tour. The passage of the stock train was an annual event at divisional points and towns where there was a stop long enough for a run to a cafe.

Life on the circuit was a procession of busy days and nights, all pointed towards the significant day in each week — the one on which the best animals in the west were led into the ring for appraisal by the judges. All through the night before, Bill and his companions would be up washing and brushing and combing their entries, the better to show their winning qualities. And when they won over the Harry Hays farm an evening of celebration was mandatory. On off days Bill and his friends kept busy tidying their quarters, on the off chance of copping the prize for best-kept stable, a prize that might reach $25 in larger cities. Dairymen had a source of income all their own. They sold milk by the pail to carneymen and track followers with whom they were warned never to play cards. The exhibitors quipped that they didn't make any money on the circuit, but they got their stock fed for free, and when they came home in September they returned with the satisfaction of a contribution made — because livestock was what exhibitions were about.

Here's a poker break for crews of the stock train. That's Lloyd Pickard at the left. Bill Hosford has an arm around his uncle Charlie.

That's how the directors of the Edmonton exhibition association felt. As the troops came home and the small country began to beat swords into ploughshares they had a delegation in Ottawa urging that the definition of *ploughshare* be extended to embrace *livestock sales pavilion*. Their first priority in the postwar world was a modern pavilion geared to sales, with a showring big enough for a carload of animals and stalls for 600. Toronto's Royal Winter Fair had been shut down by the war. Where getting ahead of Calgary had once been their ambition, they now took dead aim at Toronto. Ottawa was sympathetic on the ploughshare definition and after a third of a century the association had a major building project underway, which, in 1948 saw completion of a brick-and-concrete palace costing $312,000. It was a boost for morale and for agriculture and there was a fringe benefit which took everyone by surprise. Charlie Wilson, who had relinquished the presidency and become a fulltime manager, found he was managing a cultural centre.

128

Edmonton needed a concert hall for the Minneapolis Symphony, for Nelson Eddy, for Rise Stevens, for sixteen-year-old Bob Goulet, for Tommy Dorsey's big band. The Empire Theatre had been converted to the Trocadero Ballroom. The Stock Pavilion was pressed into a role now filled by the Jubilee Auditorium, and performers had to compete not only with fragrances of the barnyard but whistles of CNR trains rumbling past the back door. Erna Sack, the Viennese soprano, won a draw with the CNR by suspending her songs to trill in tune. Hazel Scott, the pianist, topped even that. As the third train roared past Miss Scott turned to her audience and inquired: "Say, when does this place get to Chicago?"

Across the gravel road from Edmonton's temple of culture stood its sport centre. With the football Eskimos still in limbo hockey was the hottest number in town and fans were swarming into the 1913 brick barn at a dollar-and-a-quarter each to see the Flyers battle Edmonton's rivals in the Western Canada Senior Hockey League. Returning veterans were still on the troop ships in 1945 when the exhibition association gambled $4,500 on a hockey franchise and hired Riley Mullen to assemble a team and stick it to the Calgary Stampeders, Lethbridge Maple Leafs, Regina Capitals and Saskatoon Quakers. An interprovincial league was heady evidence of warmer financial climate on the prairies. Not since the fabled twenties had senior teams ranged beyond their own borders in regular-season competition. Spirits were high and went higher in February 1947. The oil strike at Leduc sent confidence aloft in the manner of the balloon ascensions in which daredevil "professors" astonished turn-of-the-century fairgoers.

The discovery was a symbol of a changing luck style for the prairies, coming as it did on the heels of 133 failures by Imperial Oil going back to the twenties. Hockey fans coming out into the cold through those unforgettable banging doors of the Arena could see a constant reminder flaring against the night clouds in the southern sky. Alberta was nobody's poor relation anymore. In the spring of 1946 the team of the Calgary exhibition association brought home the Allan Cup, second most prestigious trophy in all of hockey, outshone only by Lord Stanley's.

And 1948 was to be the turn of the team sponsored by the Edmonton fair board. The Flyers beat back all challengers, including that of the easterners, the Ottawa Senators, and brought Sir Hugh Allan's silver chalice to the old brick barn. Over the years Edmonton fans have identified with great teams in football, girls basketball, international swimming and hockey, but with none more intensely than the boys of spring in 1948. Coach Frank Currie, goalkeeper Al Rollins on his way up to Toronto, centre Morey Rimstad on his way back from St. Louis, Pug Young and Gordie Watt the defensemen, Handy Andy Clovechok, scoring hero of the spring, and the Receding Hair Line of Kreller, Pringle and Smitten. The total payroll for this charismatic crew was $47,500, including playoffs. All regular season games were sellouts. Under pressure of fans clamoring for admittance the association was spurred to its second major building project of the postwar. An extension of the south end cost $163,000, added 12 hundred seats and a new curved facade. Though the doors still banged there was room for twelve ticket sellers in the entrance instead of six. It was altogether so impressive that a new name was required and the Arena became the Edmonton Gardens.

1950-1951

SPORTS REVIEW

EDMONTON GARDENS

10¢

GORDIE WATT

H.W.J. MADDISON
PRESIDENT

GORDON McDONALD
CHAIRMAN, HOCKEY COMMITTEE

L.M. RYE
VICE-PRESIDENT

F. W. KEMP

JAMES PAUL
MGR.-DIR.

R. "BARNEY" STANLEY

EDMONTON FLYERS HOCKEY COMMITTEE

As one set of workmen put finishing touches on the Gardens another was clearing the site for major project number three. Over at the racetrack the old wooden grandstand was coming down to make way for a thing of steel-and-concrete, rising seventy feet in two tiers, stretching 336 feet along the track, costing one-and-a-half million dollars, and designed to hold eight thousand racing fans. "Edmonton to Lead Nation with Ultra Modern Track Grandstand," reported a proud Edmonton Bulletin. Although the forty-year old stand was going down its best timbers were to rise again immediately on the east side of Clarke Stadium. The football Eskimos were being revived and a wooden stand capable of seating 35 hundred fans was required to complement the one on the west side. It had to be up for season opening on Labour Day, and it was. However, the builders of the exhibition's steel-and-concrete monument couldn't get the roof on in time for the fair of 1950. So the traditional grandstand show was held in the Gardens — a super extravaganza, said the Ex, the world's biggest indoor review, featuring the Underseas Disappearing Water Ballet.

The next year the community moved to revive another tradition of the fair. Once again it opened with a parade. The parade marshal was one of the community's doughtiest movers, John Michaels, founder of Mike's News Stand. "It will be a brilliant display of color and novelty and interest," Mike told the press. Mike and his pals had collected a thousand dollars' prize money for winning floats, and the provincial department of economic affairs had donated $200 for the best smalltown bands among the seven in that category. 133 entries took ninety minutes to pass a given point, the most sought-after point-of-vantage being the CPR bridge at Jasper Avenue and 110th Street. The crowd on the bridge was so dense that a CPR train was late leaving the depot. The parade opened with a roar, a flypast of a jet fighter and four Mitchell bombers of the City of Edmonton 418 Squadron, able to fly very low because of the two-storey buildings along Jasper. The Journal commented: "The air force's contribution of five planes which roared back and forth over the parade route was not appreciated by the horses bearing the group depicting the United Nations. Each time the planes roared overhead the horses made a sudden about-turn, throwing the U.N. into some disunity."

Under a banner headline the Journal crowed: "The first parade in twelve years, Edmonton's magnificent display of color on foot, horseback and wheels was watched by the largest crowd since V-J Day." The biggest and blackest of type proclaimed the crowd to be 100,000. Now, guessing the number of heads in a mob is the least exact of all sciences and the estimate so brazenly blazoned was surely the stuff which made balloon ascents possible at summer fairs long ago. The figure was really Edmonton's estimate of itself. In a few swift years it had gone from the thinking of a market town to that of a big city. And the thinking was reflected in all its institutions, including the exhibition.

Some champions parade past the new grandstand.

22 1951-56 A New Era

Attitudes of the city began to dominate where city and country met. A noticeable drift set in — like a current in broad waters — towards diversions for an urban population. An early sign was a requirement about animals. Animals were expected to be performers. It had once been enough for the champion bull King of the Fairies to parade solemnly past the grandstand to the cheers of the crowd. That was when the spectators were no more than a generation off the farm and understood the contribution the King was making to the quality of life. But the new attitude was "Don't just stand there, do something."

The association tried to pep up the animal acts, in three separate enterprises involving horses. They tried chuckwagon chases, a rodeo, and harness racing.

Today the association sponsors seventy-seven days a year of the harness sport, on which shrewd appraisers of horseflesh invest twenty-five million dollars and get twenty-two million back. But the initial experiment offered no hope of such a happy ending.

Bill Connelly undertook to revive racing in the mode for which the track had been designed in the first place. Bill had no experience with trotters and pacers other than as a very young spectator at the old Southside Athletic Grounds but the spectacle created a lifelong interest. He'd become a shareholder in his teens, when share number 68, issued to founder Sandy Larue, was transferred to him. By the 1950s he was a director of the exhibition, and also of the Eskimos, a football team long on fans and victories but short on cash. He persuaded the Eskimos to sponsor a harness meet to raise funds, but when the club backed off he got the exhibition to try it — a two-day meet on the Victoria Day weekend of 1952. Some forty horses were rounded up and they went to the post on such a beautiful holiday that the programs and hot dogs were gone by the third heat, and the football club lost a profit of $2,100. However, next year the meet went four days and the association took a loss of $3,400. That was the end of harness racing as far as the association was concerned. It lay in limbo until the 1960s when it was revived with such success (by a private company started by Bill Connelly) that the Ex bought back the rights.

The chuckwagons had a longer run, three seasons all told. And though they were no less rowdy and rousing than at the Calgary Stampede, this was the Edmonton exhibition. Chuckwagons in thunderous contest, outriders in full whoop-and-holler, express "the natural genius" of Calgary and the foothills, but they are foreign to Edmonton, alien as the war dances of Kirghiz tribesmen. Edmontonians were intrigued but not involved. The chuckwagons were ditched in anticipation of a really big show in 1955.

That was to be a year of banners and bunting, marking the golden anniversary of the province of Alberta, and the directors could see a mammoth historical pageant, of the kind which had one stirred the blood of grandstand patrons. They saw a production involving 15 hundred costumed citizens, costing $40,000, and contacted an American theatrical outfit about putting it on. Since it was to be in honor of the province a generous contribution was expected from that direction, and the provincial treasurer said he felt honored all right but only to the tune of $5,000.

Later on, the idea led to an indoor pageant in the Gardens — written by Elsie Park Gowan and dedicated to the founders of Edmonton — called who Builds A City. But the anniversary show of 1955 featured the Duke of Paducah, an original star of the Grand Ol' Opry. There was, to be sure, an added attraction for first nighters. On stage to declare the fair officially in business was the mayor of Montreal. Mayor Jean Drapeau, who else?

Harness racing didn't take, chuckwagons didn't belong, but the rodeo worked. It took hold and led to the Canadian Western Superodeo of 1979, which drew 50,000 fans to Northlands Coliseum. Number One was organized for the association by the famed Alberta entrepreneur of whoop-and-holler, Herman Linder of Cardston. It was scheduled for the third week in June, to lure cowboys wishing to sharpen their skills for the big shows of late summer. And it took place in front of the grandstand, because rodeos and stampedes were intended for the great outdoors. Herman explained how a rodeo differed from a stampede. There was more comedy, more roping, more entertainment — and in that department he brought in the Gene Autry Show from Hollywood.

The first production lost $7,000 through two days of rain, but next year the weather was so bad it solved the weather problem once and for all. To avert disaster the show was moved indoors — into the Gardens — and a loss of $20,000 was turned to a neat profit of $3,000. The Ex got the message. With outdoor events people wouldn't commit themselves to tickets until the weatherman made a commitment. The directors moved that the rodeo continue though the organizer would "make a concerted effort to make the show more colorful."

The urge for "color" led to contracts for a long line of TV personalities: Rex Allen, Chuck "Gunsmoke" Connors, Lorne "Pa Cartwright" Greene, Michael "Little Joe" Landon and Dan "Hoss" Blocker. And the urge soon put the rodeo committee on collision course with the spring horse show people. In 1956 there was a move to combine the two events — pep up both and attract more paying customers. The spring show people came at full gallop to state their undying opposition and the merger did not go through, but in giving his opinion that the horse show must go on in traditional manner, Lee Williams said — perhaps for the last time anyone ever said or thought it — "Primarily we are an agricultural society."

The word *primarily* was no longer operative. Everywhere strong new forces were shifting traditional balances. While the city boomed country population declined. Strong new personalities entered into the councils of the exhibition, led by Edmonton's mayor of the 50s, Bill Hawrelak. When the new breed of young city dwellers heard the motto Where City And Country Meet the country that came to mind was Canada. That was the how Mayor Drapeau happened to be riding in the parade and opening the fair.

While still an alderman in 1951 Bill Hawrelak was involved in starting up the exhibition parade for yet another time. The association put $6,000 into the revival and from that year forward was engaged in an annual contest with Calgary. There was, of course, competition for the largest "estimated" crowd and Edmonton had the advantage of coming afterwards, but there was also competition in the matter of a theme. Calgary could re-run its "wild west" theme every year but Edmonton needed a variety and this quest led eventually to Klondike Days. There was competition too for celebrities to ride past the "estimated" crowds and declare the festivities officially open. In 1952, Edmonton tried for Donald Gordon, president of the CNR, but Mr. Gordon sent regrets — he was getting married and was off to London for the coronation. Sonja Henie rode in the parade in 1954, when her ice show was a week-long attraction at the Gardens. Another time a bid was made for

It's 1954 and the parade celebrates seventy-five years of the Exhibition and fifty years of the City of Edmonton.

Ed Sullivan, the reigning king of television — Edmonton had acquired TV in 1954. Ed was too busy organizing "really big shews" but a delightful and appropriate substitute was Marilyn Bell, the Toronto girl who had captured Canadian hearts by swimming Lake Ontario. Marilyn was sponsored by the Canadian Milk Foundation, and this made a nice connection with the Boys and Girls Farm Camp, which was held on the grounds each fair week.

Alberta was in a state of rapid transit, reaching so quickly for the future that it often found one foot in the past. The exhibition association was in such a state in 1954, the year the parade theme was the 75th Anniversary of that faroff agricultural display at the Fort. Edmonton was becoming a big city but still had its dogpound on the exhibition grounds. The directors asked plaintively that it be moved. Though no longer *primarily* an agricultural society the Ex had a problem which piled up and plaintive residents near 116th Avenue and 73rd Street wondered why it must all be piled along the east fence. The board decided that the Livestock Sales Pavilion didn't provide quite the proper ambience for the Minneapolis Symphony or artists of the Celebrity Concert Series so they bought 315 yards of material, hung it from the rafters of the Gardens and created the Edmonton Gardens Concert Hall. This setting prompted a rhetorical question from French soprano Lily Pons: "What do you think I am? A circus performer?" They also bought a wooden dance floor for the Gardens but found it rough and badly in need of polishing. So they invited the local square dance clubs to a free jamboree, the Ex to supply the wax, the dancers to polish the floor with their nimble feet. The scheme worked nicely but when the dancers wanted to put on their own jamboree at a reduced rent they were told rather stiffly that they could have it on the same terms as anyone else.

By 1954 the Gardens were booked nearly ninety days a year, enough work for a fulltime manager who could promote more, so a call went out to the man most qualified — the CNR station agent at Viking. Laurie Rasmussen was the name. Laurie ran the only covered rink in small-town Alberta. As mayor of Viking he had raised the money for the arena by a scheme highly original, highly effective, though, alas, highly illegal in the puritan province of the time. He'd organized a ten-dollar ten-car raffle which brought money from all over Alberta, through the mail. "Raz" was the obvious man to run the Gardens. Legend has it that he had to be contacted by phone because the post office had suspended his mailing privileges.

Laurie joined a staff of about a dozen. Managing director was Jim Paul, who had succeeded Charlie Wilson in 1948. Jim had a large farm at Namao, and also held a unique niche in the economic history of the city. He gained his place back in 1913, a new lad in town, performing miscellaneous jobs at Colonel Jim Ramsay's department store, later sold to Eaton's. Retail transactions were conducted to the nearest nickel. By common consent the cumbersome penny was not used. But, to further such merchandising ploys as 9-cent days the Colonel decided to break with tradition. He ordered his bank to bring in a load of pennies and on the appointed day Jim Paul was despatched with a wheel-barrow to fetch the coppers.

Jim's assistant was Fred Miller. Fred had joined the staff in 1949 but he had worked with the association before that. As District Agriculturist Fred had helped arrange field days on the farm of Jim's neighbor, Ed. Clarke. Barbara Bannerman was the secretary — for the Ex and the breeder associations. Muriel Garr handled cash and correspondence for all. Jim Davison was the accountant. There was the grounds superintendent, Tom McCauley, and four or five workmen according to the season. Malcolm MacCrimmon was the icemaker in the Gardens, and therefore had the most direct and personal contact with the association's highest-

Lady champions in two departments.

paid contract employee, the able and affable Norman Robert (Bud) Poile, coach of the Flyers.

These Flyers were professionals — from the Detroit Redwing organization. The Saskatoon fair board had an arrangement with the Rangers and Calgary with the Blackhawks. The Edmonton board had opted for professionalism in 1951, feeling that senior amateur hockey was no longer of sufficient calibre for the oil capital of Canada, and there was a merger with pro teams on the coast. In amateur days of Allan Cup glory the hockey committee had been limited to lining up jobs for players who wanted to come to Edmonton, making a final offer of eighty dollars a week to Pug Young, or reimbursing the director who had paid the fine of a player who absorbed too much of "the product" after a game in Lethbridge and landed in the municipal penalty box.

But in 1951 this all changed and the committee could deal with the real pros of the National Hockey League, that philanthropic organization which took Edmonton's entire team in 1926 for expansion into eastern American cities, and in 1979 let Edmonton celebrate the centennial of the exhibition by paying six million dollars to join the league. The committee soon learned about the pros. As Jim Paul put it sadly after a meeting with Detroit's general manager, Jolly Jack Adams: "It doesn't seem fair that Mr. Adams should have all the say and we have to put up all the money."

Jim's successor, Al Anderson, got the better of the Redwings eventually, but Al's background was not in agriculture. It was in the business side of sport, and at the time he was approached to take the exhibition job was general manager of the Eskimos, a football team en route to a third straight Grey Cup, sparked by great players Al had signed. He made a special trip all the way to Mississippi to sign the greatest, and as Jackie Parker recalled the episode: "When that big guy got out of that big car with that big white hat I thought he must own Canada."

The move to bring Edmonton's top football executive into the manager's office in the Gardens came as a surprise, and a disturbing one to directors who had considered Fred Miller the obvious heir-apparent to Jim Paul. A break with the expected is always difficult even when it's not complicated by intense personal feelings and these were certainly present. Al and Fred were good friends and had worked together on a number of causes. Fred was respected by all, no less by the slim majority of directors who felt compelled towards the unexpected.

They had a feeling, a feeling one might get standing at First and Jasper watching all the cars go by, or sitting in city council listening to development applications, or squishing through the spring mud of new subdividions, or watching oil refineries flare against night clouds in the east. The feeling concerned survival of the exhibition association. Survival could only be achieved by rapid expansion. The exhibition must move, not in a different direction, but in a larger dimension. Though a non-profit organization, it would have to be run like a big business. Agriculture was still the basic industry of northern Alberta but the farm belt was taking on an urban life style and the countryside could not be served by livestock shows alone. This was the feeling.

Though not *primarily* so the organization was still an agricultural society. It had to be to continue to enjoy provincial grants and a monopoly on horseracing. That word came direct from Premier Manning, when, sometime later he was called, in effect, to play arbitrator in a dispute between stockmen and racemen. The argument arose over the annual rebate of pari-mutuel revenue. The government was in the habit of turning back to the association $50,000 of its share. The racing people argued that since their thoroughbreds earned the money it should be spent on racing facilities. Director Bill Muir went as a delegation to the premier's office to get the government's view and it was highly definite. The grant was for agriculture and the race monopoly was for service to agriculture.

The slim majority of directors who had the feeling about Al Anderson also had the feeling about stock shows and realized how important Fred Miller's expertise would continue to be. Al knew something of defensive tackles who are sometimes described as "beef on the hoof" but that knowledge wasn't nearly enough. Fred was invited to make an offer which the Ex couldn't refuse and he stayed on as assistant general manager in charge of farm events for fifteen years.

141

Having gained a football manager the directors then set about losing a hockey team. They decided that if Mr. Adams wanted all the say about the Flyers he could use his own money. Impressed, perhaps by the novelty of the idea, Mr. Adams went along with it. The Redwings took over direct operation, and as mere landlords to the Flyers, the exhibition people turned their full attention to their other club, an orphan junior team they'd adopted in 1954 after the death of car dealer Jim Christiansen, a team which eventually had its name inscribed twice on the Memorial Cup, and would, until the coming of the WHA be Edmonton's *official* hockey team.

The Oil Kings were unique. A generation of Edmonton fans lived their most impressionable and hence most memorable years sharing the destinies of the Ullmans, Bucyks, MacGregors, Quinns and Hamiltons who won the west six years in a row and won the Memorial Cup in 1963 and '66. Other fair boards, through the historical accident of having the biggest barn in town, sponsored hockey teams but the Oil Kings were something else. They served the Edmonton exhibition association as principal public relations vehicle in country towns. For a time the Kings played in a senior league with teams from Ponoka, Drumheller, etc. They also helped promote sporting activities and facilities in the towns. When city and country met it was at exhibition hockey games, ball games in summer, fund raising dinners and minor hockey weeks.

The Oil Kings were sold eventually to Bill Hunter who led them to continued success. In the 50s Bill was willing to manage the team (on behalf of the Ex) for $6,000 a season, but the hockey committee turned down Bill's perfectly reasonable offer because of an absurd offer from Leo LeClerc. Leo did it for nothing, as a hobby to go with his job on the Yellow Pages of the city telephone book. On road trips Leo paid the bills with his Diners Club card, and on one very important trip the practice brought a nervous long-distance call from the Diners' head office. The Kings were in Toronto challenging for the Memorial Cup. When charges mounted to $22,000 Leo's creditor phoned the exhibition office to make sure the account would be made good.

It took Al Anderson a long time to get the better of the Redwings, but it was achieved in 1963, the first year Edmonton ever won the Memorial Cup. The quest ended at the Gardens with Detroit general manager Syd Abel on hand counting the house and watching the Kings beat Bernie Parent, Derek Sanderson and the Niagara Falls Flyers. Detroit owned all the players and had been contributing $3,500 a season to the operation which meant that the exhibition association was subsidizing the NHL. But for this season Al had offered a new deal: no money up front, just pick up the loss if it should happen to go beyond $20,000. But the Wings failed to take into account that the association had a dual relationship with the Oil Kings — both landlord and tenant. Al played to the dastardly hilt the role of gouging landlord. It is said that Jack Adams' successor almost fell off his chair when shown a deficit of $40,507.

While scoring on Detroit was cause for chortling, it was more important to get the better of another problem — one which had been growing for a long time, for half a century in fact, ever since the fair jumped to the east end swamp and marked the site with wooden buildings. The manufacturers building, and the stables were showing symptoms of old age. Five fires in three years took the lives of a stablehand and five race horses, and destroyed 100 stalls. Since 75 percent of the association's operating surplus came from racing the board decided to protect its sources. When the horses moved out after the fall meet of 1959 contractors cleared away the wooden relics and moved in with steel, concrete and brick to raise a complex housing 800 thoroughbreds and 125 people on the level above. Cost was $1.3 million, financing supplied by the city of Edmonton's traditional bank, the Imperial, at the prime lending rate of 5¼ percent.

Racing reflected trends of the time. One trend was an increase in leisure and of money to enjoy it. Another trend was the suburban shopping centre which affected the sport in Edmonton, Calgary, Regina and Saskatoon. The shopping centre was in none of these places but in Winnipeg where Jim Speers, grand mandarin of prairie racing, had died. Jim owned Polo Park, which the estate sold to a developer keen to introduce the latest thing in bargain-and-sale. That left Winnipeg without a track, the prairie circuit without a key member, and the historic Canadian Derby without a home. So the Derby was moved to Edmonton in 1957 under protection of the exhibition association and has been further protected by copyright. All things bright and beautiful surround such an event, even to the young ladies who festoon the winner's circle. The breakfast became so prestigious that the Petroleum Club offered to admit a horse to its staid premises in an effort to lure the breakfast away from the Macdonald Hotel. Then in 1961 harness racing returned. Undaunted by disappointments of 1952 and '53 Bill Connelly built up an organization of horsemen who favored the traditional mode. With persistence and diplomacy he got two private bills through the legislature, incorporating the Northern Alberta Trotting and Pacing Association and a twin in the south. With each charter went the right to stage fourteen days of harness racing and fourteen with thoroughbreds. So the exhibition leased the facilities to the harnessmen for fifteen years — in return for one percent of the mutuel take and the extra days of thoroughbreds.

1960 saw the beginning of the end for the ancient and honorable manufacturers building, and some stalls gaped empty in its last days as exhibitors of long tenure ruled out refurbishing their crumbling locations. Replacing the landmark was to cost $2½ million, and with the bank's prime lending rate going to 5¾ percent the amount could hardly be spent on a facility good four or five times a year. A multipurpose, multi-season concept was required, and this concept produced the Sports Exhibit Building, the Sportex, with curling ice to bridge the gaps between trade fairs and boat shows. The Sportex also provided a wing for the growing administration.

Another building, more impressive than the Sportex or the giant stable, was in the minds of the shareholders. A Coliseum Committee was formed and met on August 7 1962. But that's another story. When that committee held its first meeting at the Glenora Club the quest for a theme had almost reached home.

This was a theme to unify the attractions of the fair and identify the city — as the wild west did for Calgary. An inkling of the eventual theme was given in 1959 when the Edmonton exhibition helped to celebrate Canada's golden anniversary of powered flight. The fair itself held a niche in the half-century of progress aloft. In 1918 Katherine Stinson had thrilled the grandstand crowd by landing on the infield with the first sack of airmail in western Canada. After a diligent search the heroine of '18 was found living in New Mexico and she rode in the parade and looked up in awe as the RCAF Golden Hawks whistled past the grandstand in ear-splitting precision. The week also featured a salute to the bush pilots, Edmonton's pioneer link with the north.

143

North. That was the direction the search for a theme was leading. A number of people got the message in a number of ways. Al Anderson was in Arizona on a winter holiday and each time the cheerful man on the radio gave the temperature he'd say it was so many delicious degrees *in the Valley of the Sun.* Why shouldn't Edmonton brag about its connection with the north in the same way? Calgary had first claim on the west. Let Calgary have the west. Edmonton's province was the north.

In 1960 the theme was The Modern Trend, which had little sub-Arctic flavor, but then the city of Edmonton adopted a helpful slogan: The Heart of Canada's Great North West. The slogan was adopted as the theme of the parade and exhibition of 1961. At a board meeting Al advanced the possibility of a revolving northern theme, something like a Chinese calendar. The Year of the Ox had just begun and would be followed by the Horse and other fauna until the Ox came around again. Perhaps Edmonton could have a Year of the Miner, a Year of the Bush Pilot and so on until the Miner came up again.

Northern style mining was a feature of the '61 fair. Patrons could pan for gold in sand salted with nuggets supplied by Mike Finland of the Chamber of Mines.

It was rather like a guessing game in which players uncover clues and each time work closer to a hidden answer. The answer may pop up in any circumstance or surrounding. In this case it was found at 20 thousand feet in the night sky between Edmonton and Chicago. An Edmonton delegation had been to the annual meeting of North American fair people, to meet their counterparts and the agents for show business names which would, for a price, appear before summer grandstands. They were flying home aboard a Northwest Airlines DC-6, and since there was hardly anyone else on the plane they were able to carry on a business meeting. Reg Easton was chairman, along with Roy Marler, Graham Jones, Lloyd Wilson and Al Anderson. Perhaps the airliner's ultimate destination was a clue. It was bound for Japan, by way of Alaska. They had analyzed all the fairs of North America in cities of middle size and found that the fair which made the most impact for its city was Calgary's. And it wasn't because of the show or the city. They key was citizen participation. How could they apply the principle to Edmonton? Somewhere in flight someone hit on a two-word label for a package of fun and games. The winter was harsh with many reminders of Edmonton's proximity to the north. The exhibition's parade committee liked the label on the package and it went into the record for the first time at a meeting on April 16, 1962. The parade program was adopted including a one-line item:

"THEME WILL BE KLONDIKE DAYS."

24 Klondike Days

Klondike Days was not quite a case of spontaneous combustion. Not quite, but close. It was intended as a theme for one occasion, but when members of the attractions committee gathered for the first meeting of 1963 they decided it must "continue indefinitely." Then, on February 14, they decided to go to town with the idea. Move off the exhibition grounds, and go through the city like the Irish lady with the cockles and mussels, selling Klondike Days. Make it a party, a dress-up party creating a northern image for the Edmonton district, a party in which arriving airliners and passenger trains would be met in the Klondike spirit. A downtown committee was formed with one of downtown's best-known figures as chairman — Ross McLean, manager of the menswear department at Eaton's.

Time was short. Some directors were against the idea. Downtown, many predicted failure, including this writer, who sought to persuade Leo LeClerc that Edmonton's characteristic reticence would not permit such extrovert levity, and, historically, that the city was only the third-best place to start for the Klondike, a very poor third to Vancouver and Seattle. We doubters were wrong of course, and, as for history, perhaps Great Uncle Dan Cashman filed a claim of sorts on that part of the country. Great Uncle Dan set out from here, had to turn back, and made it through Vancouver, but when he left Toronto he gave the forwarding address: Dan Cashman, Dawson City, Yukon Territory, Edmonton.

Defying the doubters, the Ex made the first investment in Klondike costumes — $500 for gamblers vests, and they were given to TV personalities, bus drivers, aldermen and other boosters in the public eye. The fair still ran six days, so the Downtowners set out to create Klondike excitement in the days leading up. A festive occasion needs a queen. To establish a line of royalty for this occasion there was a natural. On the Saturday evening before, a Klondike Kate Ball was held at the Prince of Wales Armory, and Kate the First was crowned.

For Sunday afternoon the Downtowners had the luck to acquire another natural — authentic as it was rousing, a gold rush equivalent of wild west chuckwagons, proven practical and fun on the local river. For two summers the event had been a private contest organized for their own amusement by employees of the city light and water department, a raft race to the Groat Bridge. With civic spirit the civic employees agreed to let the exhibition take over their party as the Sourdough River Race. The course was extended from Devon to the Low Level Bridge, and there was wild talk of making the winner ride a burro to an official finish line at First and Jasper. This was dropped but the committee did engage three burros (with their handlers) at $350 to parade around the city centre rigged for prospecting.

The sourdough race was a barrel of laughs and on Monday a mariner with very serious credentials rode at the head of the parade. Inspector Larson of the RCMP was skipper of the St. Roch, first ship to sail from one coast of Canada to the other through the Arctic Ocean.

In winter the junior chamber of commerce kept the Klondike theme warm with a week of frosty frolic known as Mukluk Mardi Gras. The Mardi Gras was immensely successful, so immense it eventually became too much for the Jaycees to sustain, but it was fun while it lasted and confirmed civic support for the northern idea.

Director George Prudham (who'd been an alderman and federal cabinet minister) urged that more publicity be given to livestock events in 1964 but public attention was directed to the fun side and slogans like Percherons For Power drew less response than a new symbol of gold rush frolic, a cartoon character called Klondike Mike. Mike came on the scene like an echo of Charlie Chaplin's tramp, wistfully optimistic, away on a great adventure, smiling shyly to prevent his natural timidity from creeping up on him.

Mike was developed by an ad agency artist with a name now found on expensive pictures. The name is Len Gibbs. When Len and Dave Wright (PR man for the Ex) defined Mike's character they still had to establish his occupation. How indicate that he was not a cowboy nor a lumberjack nor a roughneck who worked in the oilfields? They tried a number of ideas and then hit on the shovel. A prospector would have a shovel. So Len gave him one to lean on and he was ready for Klondike Days.

In addition to Mike, the Six Sleepy Sourdoughs came to the aid of the party in '64. The name was their choice, possibly because their project meant getting up for breakfast, probably because it meant being up in time to host a fancy-dress breakfast for two thousand converts to Klondike Days. Reg Easton was Sleepy Sourdough Number One. Reg had just become past-president of the Ex and decided that the week should have a Klondike version of the Harry Hays breakfast which ushered in the Calgary Stampede. Senator Hays gave every possible assistance to the Edmonton cause. Three men put on his breakfast. Reg figured he'd need twice that many, and that was the rationale for Six Sleepy Sourdoughs. Dennis Yorath became number two and when Dennis observed that Tommy Fox's farm in Whitemud Creek would be a fine location for the breakfast Tommy became the third. Jack Weber, Fred Jenner and Cec Ross completed the roster, and, showing the "town aspect," only Reg and Cec were involved in the exhibition association. Refreshments were donated for the inaugural breakfast — except for the twelve cases of gin and the butter for the pancakes. How would you find out it's illegal to donate butter unless you put on a Sourdough Breakfast? Eventually the breakfast became so sucessful and so big the volunteer sourdoughs could no longer maintain it, but another downtown feature survived handsomely. Walterdale Playhouse staged their first Klondike Melodrama at the Strand Theatre with Wally McSween as the villain and Judy Unwin as the girl who was TEMPTED TRIED AND TRUE. And Unwin is a name to be recognized here. No one person did more to promote downtown entertainment than Judy's father, the late Jack Unwin.

Klondike entertainment required a beat, a beat distinct and apart from the twangity-thump of Stampede guitars. The honkytonk piano was clearly the instrument to provide it but that mode of playing was something of a lost art, except with American recording stars like Johnny Maddox. So to sound the beat and demonstrate the art the great Maddox was imported for a week and paid $800. It was recognized that the demands on Klondike Kate could be met only by a rugged disciplined professional able to belt out vibrant songs morning noon and night. So Toni Carroll became the first imported Kate. However, the Klondike-minded were now thinking in terms of *export* rather than *import*. In their keenness they even suggested that Klondike might invade the dollhouses of the world. Maybe Cee Dee Toys, inventor of the Barbie Doll, would outfit Barbie and Ken with Klondike costumes.

147

Al Anderson and old-time band whoop it up for Klondike Days while Jack Unwin takes a smoke break. Klondike Mike indicates he's ready to roll.

Thinking had jumped far beyond "the town aspect" of 1962. The downtown committee became a Theme Promotion Committee, sparked by vigorous Bill Jackson of the CNR (no relation to the talk show host who was later employed by the Ex). In 1965 the Theme group took a permanent office in the business district and became the Klondike Days Association. In recent years the Ex and K-Days people have not always seen eye to eye but this is a common parent-offspring relationship.

The northern theme pervaded the grounds as well. Klondike Village was designed to "depict with authenticity the life and times of a western Canadian town during and after the 1890s and early 1900s." The miniature train ride took an authentic name from steam train history: Edmonton Yukon and Pacific, a railway which started in Strathcona and reached only its first objective. The Food Service Building became the Golden Garter. What may have been the first casino in Canada ran in The Silver Slipper. The ancient Gardens acquired yet another alias — Klondike Palace. And in 1963 a big sign reading NORTHLANDS went up on the grandstand. In centennial year the exhibition association put the name Northlands on the entire operation.

Bigger names entertained at the grandstand. The Smothers Brothers. Rosemary Clooney. Rich Little. Jack Benny. And the Ex was able to land some big names to ride in the parade. Prime Minister Lester Pearson was the catch of 1967, Canada's centennial year. He opened only one fair and it was ours.

Next year when food service manager George Lee was permitted to raise the price of coffee from ten to fifteen cents, some directors wanted to invite Ronald Reagan but the California governor roused opposition so they decided to get someone non-controversial and asked Joey Smallwood. Joey was too busy so they invited Nancy Greene, who had just raced to fame on the ski slopes. Nancy accepted but then came a letter from her manager. Nancy had turned pro and the fee would be $1,150. She got it.

Names from show business and statecraft became important in other events. In fact, the Governor of Hawaii was blamed for disappointing attendance at a Northwest Trade Fair. The Governor was billed for the opening ceremonies but sent late regrets. The initial trade fair was held in 1963 at the Sportex, as the ancient manufacturers building finally went down in splinters and its concrete pad was broken up to fill low spots on the grounds. The trade fair was an omen of change. In earlier times displays in the demolished building were an integral part of the summer exhibition but now so much was going on that manufacturers needed their own show on less crowded dates in April. After the trade fair, came boat and trailer shows, and more recently the Good Earth Show with an environmental twist.

The trade fair was more than a change. It was a fragmentation of the one big week when City and Country met. And fragmentation was overtaking the country side too. Though many worked earnestly and hard to maintain the position of agriculture, a telling entry is found in the minutes of the Dairy Cattle Committee. The meeting was on January 13 1970.

It was generally agreed that changes in the livestock shows are bound
to come and that shows must become consumer-oriented.

The committee merely recognized a fact of life. By 1970 they were working in an urban society. In days when the King of the Fairies led the grandstand parade the consumer was close to the farm and applauded what the King and the breeder associations were doing for beef consumers everywhere. But that era was gone. Livestock shows were increasingly separate from other events. City and Country shared the same ground but seldom met. Old Macdonald's Farm, the last token reminder to children that agriculture is the basic industry of Alberta, disappeared from the midway. And Regina, which is not a stockraising area, puts on the premiere livestock show in the west. Senior shareholders make no secret of keen regret about the prestige position slipping away to Regina. They feel that Edmonton could have had that and the other things too.

Klondike was not the only theme of the period. There was another, recurring through several intriguing variations until a satisfactory version was achieved. The theme was sounded first on August 7 1962 in a confidential conference at the Glenora Club. City officials called the meeting to discuss it and exhibition people were there because, with their experience in running the big brick barn, they were to be involved in running it. It was the Coliseum.

The city's idea was a three-for-one facility — trade centre, convention centre and hockey arena — downtown at Jasper and 98th Street, close to the Rapid Transit line, which was already a consideration. Clarence Campbell, president of the NHL, came to a meeting and recommended no more than 7,000 seats for hockey. The concept was developed by the Stanford Research Institute of California, and put to the ratepayers — and rejected. So much for Variation One.

Then in 1966 the fire marshal played his own reverse-variation on the theme — by closing the Gardens. A fire hazard, he ruled. While thinking Coliseum the city was suddenly left without even a brick barn. This would never do. City council responded with a fireproof concrete grandstand inside the ancient brick walls at a cost of $900,000. Renovation took away the steel posts, which, for half a century, had obscured the view from many seats. Renovation also took away many of the seats, and when the Gardens reopened just in time to avoid a lawsuit from Ice Capades 1967 there were only 52 hundred, fewer than in the 1920s.

As the Gardens came into second bloom the biggest of all variations on the theme was sounded. Omniplex was the title, a fourteen-storey concrete box at 97th Street and 105th Avenue, so huge it included an indoor football field on hydraulic jacks. Bill Henning, recently an alderman and president of the exhibition association, was chairman of Citizens for Omniplex, and it was again assumed that the Ex would be involved in the running. But Omniplex, like Coliseum Number One, suffered defeat at the polls.

The next variation concerned a possible site for a Coliseum and other exhibition facilities of the future. The site was Speedway Park, popular but financially-troubled auto racetrack in the northwest. The city thought Speedway might make a landbank with the Ex running it in the meantime. A study put the chill on that idea, but as it sank in defeat there came a day which belongs in the record books — the starting date for fast-moving achievement of the final variation. The date was September 13 1971. In city council this resolution was approved:

> That a committee headed by the mayor (Ivor Dent) immediately contact the senior levels of government, possibly working with other authorities, to get a definite financial commitment for recreational grants which may be used for building Omniplex or such other sports facilities as council may deem, in its wisdom, desirable.

While not exactly a shot heard 'round the world this directive was the starting gun for a high-speed achievement. The old Gardens took two years and eleven months from resolution to opening — September 10 1910 to August 11 1913. The Coliseum, vastly more complicated in every aspect, took but three years and two months — from September 13 1971 to the evening of November 10 1974 when the Edmonton Oilers faced off against the Cleveland Crusaders. In three years and two months the site was determined, land was bought, financing was confirmed at three levels — municipal, provincial and federal, the Coliseum was designed and built and the first hockey game was played.

In retrospect the ratepayers had shown wisdom in rejecting Variations One and Two. The Jasper Avenue Coliseum would have been too small for major league hockey. Omniplex would have been too small for major league football and unsuitable for the Commonwealth Games in which track and field events must be outdoors. And the Games became an immediate factor in Plan Three. A month to the day after the September resolution the federal government gave Edmonton permission to compete for host city in '78. Success would guarantee financial help for the needed facilities, including the stadium and Coliseum.

Edmonton's bid would not be made until August 1972 — in Munich. By that time plans for big new facilities would have to be far advanced; which meant that someone had to take responsibility for the Coliseum. The Exhibition Association was the logical choice, however, the Ex was heavily engaged in a long-range projection for the provincial government and did not leap to grab this $18 million tiger by the tail. But then the World Hockey Association became a factor.

One of the most-told legends of sport relates that the WHA began at Disneyland. The same can be told of the Coliseum. Early in 1972 Jack Bailey and Harry Hole and Al Anderson were in Anaheim, California, scouting grandstand talent when a phone call came from the office of Edmonton city commissioner Stan Hampton. Bill Hunter and Dr. Allard, who were putting a team in the WHA, wanted a site for an Arena in southeast Edmonton. Was the Ex prepared to build the coliseum on the grounds? The decision had to be "Let's do it!" — a decision formally recorded April 18 at a meeting of the executive and planning-and-development committees:

> Moved by Mr. Chris Graefe and seconded by Mr. Tommy Fox
> that . . . the association express to the city council its interest in pro-
> viding a 16,000 seat arena. UNANIMOUSLY CARRIED.

The motion having been carried unanimously the project was then carried forward strenuously. On August 24 1972 when Edmonton made the winning case for
hosting the Commonwealth Games, the Coliseum was rolling.

On September 12, as Bill Hunter's Oilers sweated throught their initial workouts
in the Gardens, the site was confirmed.

On October 12 the design was awarded to Phillips and Barrat, who had done
Vancouver the favor of the PNE Coliseum.

On May 26 1973 construction was awarded to Batoni and Bowlen.

And on November 10 1974 the largest crowd ever to have seen a hockey game
in Alberta, 15 thousand strong, streamed in to the building to be astounded by the
size and brilliance of it all. And the rightness of it all. So beautifully functional, the
comfortable sightlines from all seats, the wide walkways for meeting friends between periods, even the radiating roof supports which glittered high overhead like
the Aurora Borealis. For fans conditioned to the ancient Gardens the first
experience of the Coliseum was unforgettable.

Unforgettable, the Coliseum, less memorable that it was raised in three years
and two months on the initiative and drive of people for whom the achievement
offered no personal gain. Without these people, the Jack Baileys and Harry Holes,
the Coliseum would not have happened and Edmonton would not be in the NHL.

As the Coliseum mushroomed, the racetrack extended — from a half-mile to
five-eights, and thereby hangs a chronic contention. The Edmonton exhibition
association, as already noted, is one of the few in North America to have a pony
connection, which has come under periodic fire since 1903 when the Bulletin
defended racing for the lively spell it cast on the fair.

The track takes room, as seen in the aerial view of Northlands, and all that space
is reserved for a mere three percent of the population. Events like the Canadian
Derby draw large casual crowds but surveys taken by the Ex indicate that a hard
core of fifteen thousand bettors support racing, and support is unfailingly
generous. Fascinating human beings abound among them, spiritual descendants of
track followers about whom racing manager Morris Taylor can reminisce for hours
— legends the like of Boxcar Gordie, Coast-to-Coasty and most ingenious of all,
Winnipeg's gift to the paddock area, Whittier Park Slim. But bettors don't mix
much with other patrons, as Ted Mildon noted when plans were being drawn for
Klondike Village. As chairman of the race committee Ted wrote that horseplayers
could not care less about Klondike Days but their financial contribution was important and they should not be impeded.

This raises an obvious question: Ought so much space be dedicated to a minority
who do not venerate the Klondike spirit; neither do they give a damn about the
Design for Living Show, or Alberta Farm Family Awards, or the School Art
Exhibit, or other events to which volunteers give so many earnest hours?

Then pops the owner question: Horse owners sit on the race committee and
other committees of influence. Is that a conflict of interest?

And how about the provincial government? Once upon a time the province did
the Ex a favor by letting it manage racing — and did racing a favor too because the
sport could not have survived otherwise. But now that the sport of kings and
queens is so healthy that private enterprise would gladly take over, it's clearly con-
venient for the province to have a service club do the work. In the favor department, is the horseshoe now on the other foot?

The question of who is getting the favor is a new one but the one about the owners has been around a long time and the two answers are the same, depending on perception. From the outside it may well seem a too-cosy arrangement, horselovers able to aid and abet their hobby by influencing a public body. From the inside view, the race committee is not a regulatory body. It is there to develop racing, which is deemed to be advantageous overall, and the owners contribute practical knowledge to realistic decisions.

As to the deference shown the Whittier Park Slims: The bettors contribute in two ways. They patronize the lounges and concessions on 156 days. This allows a balanced continuous operation over a full year. On race days bettors in 1978 produced a profit of $330,000. At the mutuels they wagered $73 million of which one percent or $730,000 was the provincial tax. This came back as a grant for a total of $1,060,000 equal to the carrying charges on the Coliseum.

The average citizen, trying to make a satisfactory personal judgment on whether *his* exhibition association ought to be running horses, is further confused by shifting attitudes towards gambling. Governments which once doled out bingo permits on tight strings — and stopped Laurie Rasmussen's mail for raffling cars in aid of the Viking Arena — have gone into big cash lotteries. Loto Canada and the Western Canada Lottery have contributed $1,850,000 each towards the cost of the Coliseum. It was the gaming connection which caused police and revenue agents to make their nocturnal raid of 1975 at the Edmonton fairground, rather than Winnipeg, Regina or Calgary. The police moved through the fair grabbing all the records, and citizens who perceived the Ex with mistrust nudged their neighbours and said "Ah ha! We knew it all the time." But the target was Royal American Shows, suspected of holding back on its dues to governments and the exhibition association. In other cities Royal American held a gaming concession on a flat fee, but in Edmonton there was a percentage split so the swoop was conducted here.

Though the raid was sudden the aftermath was lengthy and confusing, three years including a judicial inquiry dealing largely with disputes which flared up after the raid, disputes to which the association was not party. At the end Mr. Justice Laycraft concluded that there had been no fraud against the exhibition. The only disquieting result was the early retirement of Al Anderson.

In '76 Conklin Shows replaced Royal American on the midway, and a new general manager came from city hall. Chief commissioner George Hughes had been a member of the association's executive committee for some time and moved easily to another chair at the same conference table. And coming in as general manager number seven, George reversed an historic trend. Number one was Arthur G. Harrison, who had gone to city hall as a commissioner in 1912.

But history is a one-way street. There's no going back to 1912, nor to 1879 and the fair of the Edmonton Agricultural Society. Edmonton *was* an agricultural society then. It's not anymore. And if the founders could visit the centennial site they'd be enchanted by the vast Coliseum, the scientific stables and the big grandstand with glassed-in-viewing. Chief Factor Hardisty, host at Fort Edmonton for the first fair, was proud to live in the *Big House* which had the first glass windows in the northwest.

The only direction is forwards — with an association of which there are two perceptions. Seen from within as a great happy service club banded together to serve the public, it is often perceived by that public as the Magic Kingdom of Northlands, a private club beholden to nobody. Though both views are understandable the closer a person gets to the scene of the action he will incline towards perception number one.

From close up it looks little like a Magic Kingdom, and very much like an ordinary democracy — with the merits and defects of such a body. As Churchill put it: The worst possible system except for all the others. In a democratic society people volunteer their services. In 1978, when the new Northlands logo was being designed (by a man in Montreal) one committee worker proposed that the letter V be superimposed — V for Volunteer — to let the public know the energy source. Volunteers even pay their way onto the grounds in Klondike Days — the result of a long-ago conflict with the Edmonton Journal which promised to raise merry hell about an increase to 75 cents in gate admission unless members of the association had to pay too. On the matter of the logo the majority decided it should be restricted to one aim only: that the association operates a year-round integrated program of entertainment and education on a site called Northlands, a name which will identify Edmonton.

The crowd booed the logo when it was unveiled at the hockey game. Booing the logo is one way to exert influence on the course of human events in a democratic society, though less effective than getting involved in the work. Involvement is not difficult. Let us count the ways.

Quick way: Work on a committee. Get an annual report. Choose a committee to which you would like to contribute expertise and energy and contact the chairman. It is not necessary to be a shareholder.

Lego-Technical Way: Write to the president and apply for a share. Twice a year available shares are transferred to applicants, with priority given volunteers active on committees. A share issued in this way is a work permit. Shares are scarce, limited to two hundred by the charter of 1908. Many holders regard them as family heirlooms; three-quarters take no active part in the work so the fifty-or-so active shares mean work. A share can be revoked only if the holder misses three consecutive annual meetings. Women applicants are needed. As this was written only six of the two hundred were women.

Civic way: Next fall when the city clerk advertises in the newspapers for nominees to serve on civic boards apply to be a director of the exhibition association. Only the association can admit you to the company of shareholders, who elect twelve directors. But the city, by ancient treaty, has the right to appoint an equal number, six each year. Directors have voting power but unless you work with a committee you will exert little influence. The story is told of a civic appointee so work-resistant that he wouldn't second a motion to adjourn!

Last, and least-expected, the *Non-Volunteer Way.* Over the years many an unsuspecting citizen has been conscripted. Happily minding his own business he has looked up to a pointing finger and a face right off that famous American recruiting poster announcing: "I want YOU!" The face and commanding voice may belong to the president of the association, or a committee chairman or the general manager. Whoever and however, there is no escape. The victim's expertise in some line of human endeavor is required for a job. That job done, the victim is rewarded with a share and stays on to work at projects of his own devising.

Those are the ways to participate in shaping the destiny of the Edmonton exhibition association. And the word *participate* should be underlined. Only through wide and balanced participation by the community will consensus be regained on the purpose and potential of the exhibition idea. Only through community involvement will the association, in its second century, keep pace with the future and faith with the past.

We gratefully acknowledge the assistance provided by the following:

Cathy Philip — Researcher

Mel Hurtig — Adviser

Edith Hilton for personal recollections

Louis Hyndman — Master in Chambers — Edmonton Law Courts — Legal research

Dianne Price — Indexer

Joseph Forsyth — Director Alberta Culture Library Services

James Parker — Archivist University of Alberta

Vicky Harding — Department of Education

Glenbow — Alberta Institute

Public Archives of Canada

Provincial Archives

The City of Edmonton Archives

Alberta Culture — Historical Publication Grant

The management and staff of the Edmonton Exhibition Association

Our special 'thanks' to Mike Marples — Chairman Public Relations Committee 1977-78, whose dream of preserving the ''Magic'' and hard work made this book possible and to John Bencharsky — Chairman Public Relations Committee 1979 for seeing this project completed.

PHOTO CREDITS

Edmonton City Archives   50   51   54   55   64   69   70   75   79   82-3   85   104   106-7   115   117   121   127   133   136-7   139   152

Glenbow Alberta Institute   62   77   80   81   97   99   102   109

Provincial Archives of Alberta   20   31   45   62   92

Provincial Archives (Ernest Brown Collection)   23   40-41   44   67

Archives of Saskatchewan   26   27

Pubic Archives of Canada (Geological Survey of Canada)   6-7

Al Anderson   148

Thomas Irvine   89

Bill Hosford   128

Jim Tustian   10-11

Exhibition Association   145   148

Author's Collection   87   111   130   131

1979 BOARD OF DIRECTORS

OFFICERS

President **A.R. McBAIN**
First Vice-President **H.L.D. PERRY**
Second Vice-President **ALLAN SHENFIELD**
General Manager/Secretary **G.S. HUGHES**
Treasurer **F. JOHNSON**

EXECUTIVE COMMITTEE

A.R. McBAIN	H.L.D. PERRY
H.E. MILDON	ALLAN SHENFIELD
M.S. MARPLES	ALDERMAN L.O. OLSEN
K.C. WEBB	ALDERMAN O. BUTTI
MAYOR C.J. PURVES	

Ex-Officio Directors

CHIEF COMMISSIONER D.F. BURROWS	COMMISSIONER T.E. ADAMS
COMMISSIONER A.H. SAVAGE	COMMISSIONER P.H. WALKER

DIRECTORS

D.M. HAMILTON	M.A. AWID
JOHN BENCHARSKY	T.J. CAVANAGH
J. HIGGINS	D.D. KUCHINSKI
W.A.D. BURNS	W.F. PURDY
D.J. BUCHANAN	F. SAVAGE
M.R. COLLINS	R.W. SHOPLAND
D.B. CRAWFORD	D.H. SPRAGUE
G.W. LAVOLD	D.H. SMITH
J. SHECKTER	DR. R.C.P. WESTBURY
W. MACK	D. GOODY

HONORARY LIFE DIRECTORS

J.L. BAILEY	G.W. JONES
ROY BALLHORN	ROY C. MARLER
L.P. BROMHAM	WILLIAM MUIR
E.I. CLARKE, JR.	L.M. RYE
REG. C. EASTON	W.H. SPRAGUE
W.J.M. HENNING	J.A. WEBER
H. HOLE	LEE WILLIAMS
L.E. WILSON	

INDEX

The Next Hundred Years

TO BE CONTINUED